SOMETHING BEAUTIFUL FOR GOD

Something

Beautiful for God

Mother Teresa of Calcutta

Malcolm Muggeridge

HARPER & ROW, PUBLISHERS
New York, Evanston, San Francisco, London

All royalties from this book will be given to:
Mother Teresa's Mission of Charity (Registered
under the Charities Act 1960). UK Branch of
the International Association of Co-Workers of
Mother Teresa; Hon. Treasurer, Mr J.C. Reid,
c/o Lloyds Bank Ltd, 147 High Street, Guildford,
Surrey, England

LIBRARY OF CONGRESS CATALOG CARD NUMBER: 77-155106

12   13   14   15   16   17   18   19   20

Contents

List of Illustrations

SOMETHING BEAUTIFUL FOR GOD

CORPORATION OF CALCUTTA
NIRMAL HRIDAY
HOME FOR DYING DESTITUTES
কলিকাতা পৌর প্রতিষ্ঠান
নির্ম্মল হৃদয়
মুমূর্ষু নিরাশ্রয়দের আশ্রয়স্থান

SOMETHING
BEAUTIFUL FOR
GOD

I should explain, in the first place, that Mother Teresa has
requested that nothing in the nature of a biography or
biographical study of her should be attempted. 'Christ's
life', she wrote to me, 'was not written during his lifetime,
yet he did the greatest work on earth – he redeemed the
world and taught mankind to love his Father. The Work is
his Work and to remain so, all of us are but his instruments,
who do our little bit and pass by.' I respect her wishes in this,
as in all other matters. What we are expressly concerned with
here is the work she and her Missionaries of Charity – an
order she founded – do together, and the life they live
together, in the service of Christ, in Calcutta and elsewhere.
Their special dedication is to the poorest of the poor; a wide
field indeed.

Already they have houses in other Indian towns, in
Australia and Latin America and Rome. There are also
houses in Tanzania, Ceylon and Jordan. They are springing
up all the time, almost of themselves, wherever the chain of
affliction and destitution bites. In that Mother Teresa is the
inspirer and mainspring of this work, the one to whom all

the others turn, she has to be picked out for special attention. Pretty well everyone who has met her would agree, I think, that she is a unique person in the world today; not in our vulgar celebrity sense of having neon lighting about her head. Rather in the opposite sense – of someone who has merged herself in the common face of mankind, and identified herself with human suffering and privation.

It is, of course, true that the wholly dedicated like Mother Teresa do not have biographies. Biographically speaking, nothing happens to them. To live for, and in, others, as she and the Sisters of the Missionaries of Charity do, is to eliminate happenings, which are a factor of the ego and the will. 'Yet not I, but Christ liveth in me,' is one of her favourite sayings. I once put a few desultory questions to her about herself, her childhood, her parents, her home, when she first decided to become a nun. She responded with one of her characteristic smiles, at once quizzical and enchanting; a kind of half smile that she summons up whenever something specifically human is at issue, expressive of her own in-corrigible humanity. Her home, she said, had been an exceptionally happy one. So, when her vocation came to her as a schoolgirl, the only impediment was precisely this loving, happy home which she did not wish to leave. Of course the vocation won, and for ever. She gave herself to Christ, and through him to her neighbour. This was the end of her biography and the beginning of her life; in abolishing her-self she found herself, by virtue of that unique Christian transformation, manifested in the Crucifixion and the Resurrection, whereby we die in order to live.

There is much talk today about discovering an identity, as

though it were something to be looked for, like a winning number in a lottery; then, once found, to be hoarded and treasured. Actually, on a sort of Keynesian principle, the more it is spent the richer it becomes. So, with Mother Teresa, in effacing herself, she becomes herself. I never met anyone more memorable. Just meeting her for a fleeting moment makes an ineffaceable impression. I have known people burst into tears when she goes, though it was only from a tea party where their acquaintance with her amounted to no more than receiving her smile. Once I had occasion to see her off, with one of the Sisters, at Calcutta railway station. It was the very early morning, and the streets were full of sleeping figures; sleeping with that strange, poignant abandon of India's homeless poor. We drove up to the station, absurdly enough, in a large American limousine which happened to be at my disposal. The porters rushed expectantly forward, and then fell back disappointed when I got out followed by two nuns wearing the white saris of their order, made of the cheapest possible cloth, and carrying for luggage only a basket of provisions, most of which, I well knew, would be distributed along the way. I saw them to the train, and settled them in a third-class compartment. Mother Teresa has a pass on the Indian railways given her by the Government. She has tried very hard to get a similar pass for air travel, and at one point offered to work as an air hostess on her air journeys in return for one; a prospect that I find delectable. Unfortunately, her offer was not accepted.

When the train began to move, and I walked away, I felt as though I were leaving behind me all the beauty and all the joy in the universe. Something of God's universal love has rubbed off on Mother Teresa, giving her homely features a noticeable luminosity; a shining quality. She has lived so closely with her Lord that the same enchantment clings about her that sent the crowds chasing after him in Jerusalem and Galilee, and made his mere presence seem a harbinger of healing. Outside, the streets were beginning to stir; sleepers awakening, stretching and yawning; some raking over the piles of garbage in search of something edible. It was a scene of desolation, yet it, too, seemed somehow irradiated. This love, this Christian love, which shines down on the misery we make, and into our dark hearts that make it; irradiating all, uniting all, making of all one stupendous harmony. Momentarily I understood; then, leaning back in my American limousine, was carried off to breakfast, to pick over my own particular garbage-heap.

I should add, perhaps, that the home Mother Teresa so loved was Albanian in Yugoslavia, and that she comes of peasant stock. This is apparent in her appearance and bearing and way of looking at things. Without the special grace vouchsafed her, she might have been a rather hard, and even grasping, person. God has turned these qualities to his own ends. I never met anyone less sentimental, less scatty, more down-to-earth. Thus, until she can accommodate her lepers in proper settlements where they can live useful, productive lives together, they still go out to beg in the streets of Calcutta if they want to. 'It's interesting for them,' she explained to me. If she happens to see them when they have come back, she will ask them how they have done. Not too well, it seemed, on the day I was with her. She commiserated with them on their poor takings. It was very beautiful to see her thus so eagerly, and with so lively an interest, discussing something so near to their hearts. Saints, I reflected, are far more like Mistress Quickly than Beatrice Webb or Eleanor Roosevelt – a thought that gave me great satisfaction.

It was while she was teaching at the Loreto convent school in Calcutta that the second great break in Mother Teresa's life took place; the call within a call, as she puts it. She had occasion to go into some of the very poorest streets of Calcutta – and where are there any poorer? – and suddenly realized that she belonged there, not in her Loreto convent with its pleasant garden, eager schoolgirls, congenial colleagues and rewarding work. Again the only impediment to her new vocation was the happiness and happy relationships it required her to relinquish. It might seem strange to regard any religious order as an unduly easeful existence, but that was how Mother Teresa saw it in contrast with the lives of the very poor in Calcutta. She had to wait for some two years to be released from the vows she had already taken in order to be able to go back into the world, there to take even stricter vows of her own devising. Ecclesiastical authority, I should add, is something that she accepts in the same unquestioning way that peasants accept the weather, or sailors storms at sea. It would never occur to her either to venerate or to challenge it. So she just waited patiently. When at last her release came, she stepped out with a few rupees in her pocket, made her way to the poorest, wretchedest quarter of the city, found a lodging there, gathered together a few abandoned children – there were plenty to choose from – and began her ministry of love.

This act of superb, some would say outrageous, courage

and faith made a particularly strong impression on me when I heard tell of it. As it happened, I lived in Calcutta for eighteen months or so in the middle thirties when I was working on the *Statesman* newspaper there, and found the place, even with all the comforts of a European's life – the refrigeration, the servants, the morning canter round the Maidan or out at the Jodhpur Club, and so on – barely tolerable. Conditions then, in any case, were by no means as bad as they are today; for one thing, the refugees had not come pouring in from a newly created and ludicrously delineated Pakistan. Even so, they were bad enough, and I always thought of the city as one of the dark places of our time, where the huge fortunes made out of jute and other industries only served to pile ever higher the human debris out of which they were made. Thus, to *choose*, as Mother Teresa did, to live in the slums of Calcutta, amidst all the dirt and disease and misery, signified a spirit so indomitable, a faith so intractable, a love so abounding, that I felt abashed.

Brooding upon it, I called to mind a particular incident which had greatly affected me at the time, to the point that it sometimes came into my dreams. I was being driven one evening in my car when my driver knocked someone over – something as easily done then as now, with the crowded pavements spilling over into the roadway. With great resourcefulness, and knowing the brawls that could so easily develop when a European car was involved in a street accident, my driver jumped out, grabbed the injured man, put him in the driving seat beside him, and drove away at top speed to the nearest hospital. There, I rather self-righteously insisted on seeing that the man was properly attended to (as it turned out, he was not seriously hurt), and, being a sahib, was able to follow him into the emergency ward. It was a scene of inconceivable confusion and horror, with patients stretched out on the floor, in the corridors, everywhere. While I was waiting, a man was brought in who had just cut his throat from ear to ear. It was too much; I made off, back to my comfortable flat and a stiff whisky and soda, to expatiate through the years to come on Bengal's wretched social conditions, and what a scandal it was, and how it was greatly to be hoped that the competent authorities would . . . and so on.

I ran away and stayed away; Mother Teresa moved in and stayed. That was the difference. She, a nun, rather slightly built, with a few rupees in her pocket; not particularly clever, or particularly gifted in the arts of persuasion. Just with this Christian love shining about her; in her heart and on her lips. Just prepared to follow her Lord, and in accordance with his instructions regard every derelict left to die in the streets as him; to hear in the cry of every abandoned child, even in the tiny squeak of the discarded foetus, the cry of the Bethlehem child; to recognize in every leper's stumps the hands which once touched sightless eyes and made them see, rested on distracted heads and made them calm, brought back health to sick flesh and twisted limbs. As for my expatiations on Bengal's wretched social conditions – I regret to say that I doubt whether, in any divine accounting, they will equal one single quizzical half smile bestowed by Mother Teresa on a street urchin who happened to catch her eye.

What the poor need, Mother Teresa is fond of saying, even more than food and clothing and shelter (though they need these, too, desperately), is to be wanted. It is the outcast state their poverty imposes upon them that is the most agonizing. She has a place in her heart for them all. To her, they are all children of God, for whom Christ died, and so deserving of all love. If God counts the hairs of each of their heads, if none are excluded from the salvation the Crucifixion offers, who will venture to exclude them from earthly blessings and esteem; pronounce this life unnecessary, that one better terminated or never begun? I never experienced so perfect a sense of human equality as with Mother Teresa among her poor. Her love for them, reflecting God's love, makes them equal, as brothers and sisters within a family are equal, however widely they differ in intellectual and other attainments, in physical beauty and grace.

This is the only equality there is on earth, and it cannot be embodied in laws, enforced by coercion, or promoted by protest and upheaval, deriving, as it does, from God's love, which, like the rain from heaven, falls on the just and the unjust, on rich and poor, alike. Driving about Calcutta with Mother Teresa, I noticed that she tended to become restless and uneasy when we were passing through the more affluent districts of the town. The sight of so many buildings dedicated to other purposes, which she could use to house her poor, distressed her. At one particularly, as I recall, she positively glowered – an exceptionally ugly, ornate, but still large and solidly built, memorial to Queen Victoria set up by Curzon during his viceroyalty. It would, she said, just do for her. I wondered how the ghost of Curzon would respond to this suggestion, which, incidentally, I should not be in the least surprised to see put into execution. Back in her own part of the town, she was at ease again. Her and the Sisters' and

Brothers' identification with the poor among whom they live is no mere figure of speech. They eat the same food, wear the same clothes, possess as little, are not permitted to have a fan or any of the other mitigations of life in Bengal's sweltering heat. Even at their prayers, the clamour and discordancies of the street outside intrude, lest they should forget for a single second why they are there and where they belong.

I first met Mother Teresa in person some three years ago at a religious house near Portland Place, where I conducted a television interview with her for the BBC. All I knew about her – such as it was – I had mugged up in the train on my way to London. The interview had been set up in a great hurry thanks to the initiative of Oliver Hunkin, for which I shall be eternally grateful to him. I sat waiting for her, with appropriate questions running through my head; the camera, the lights, the sound recordist, all in position. A scene desolatingly familiar to me. Then she came in. It was, for me, one of those special occasions when a face, hitherto unknown, seems to stand out from all other faces as uniquely separate and uniquely significant, to be thenceforth for ever recognizable. Though we pursue egotistic and carnal ends with an avidity that, alas, not even advancing years can wholly cure, we yet recognize with delight the spirit that has detached itself from these purposes. What we most want, we most despise, and we yet give our hearts where our hopes and desires are most alien. So, I knew that, even if I were never to see Mother Teresa again, the memory of her would stay with me for ever. As, indeed, it surely will.

Television interviews are a sort of hypnosis. They proceed on their own momentum; afterwards, if one happens to see them, one sees and hears oneself as a total stranger – a distressing experience. The whole process is as remote from reality as one of those synthetic food products – a ham-and-eggs or steak-and-kidney pie in the form of grey anonymous particles which only need to be heated up to become the requisite dish – is from actual food. I cannot say that my interview with Mother Teresa seemed at the time any different from the general run. I put the expected questions: When did she first feel this special vocation? Any doubts or regrets? etc., etc. It would be easy to produce a little all-purpose set of questions to be used with anyone at any time. Mother Teresa's answers were perfectly simple and perfectly truthful; so much so that I had some uneasiness about keeping the interview going for the required half hour. Controversy, the substance of such programmes, does not arise in the case of those who, like Mother Teresa, are blessed with certainties. If the sun and moon should doubt, they'd immediately go out, Blake wrote. He might have added that they would also, thereby, automatically become the subject of controversy. Television's talking heads discuss interminably what they don't know, and seek to prove what they must ever doubt.

The most extreme example I ever met with of this propensity of the pure in heart to answer laconically was P. G. Wodehouse, who, when I asked him if he had ever been interested in religion, simply answered, No. Mother Teresa was almost as laconic when I asked her whether she did not think that the destitution she was trying to cope with in Calcutta required a government agency disposing of vastly greater resources of money and manpower than her Sisters of the Missionaries of Charity did or could. The more govern-

ment agencies did the better, she said; what she and the Sisters had to offer was something else – Christian love. Criticism of Mother Teresa is often directed at the insignificant scale of the work she and the Sisters undertake by comparison with the need. It is even suggested that, by seeming to achieve more than she does, or can, she may actually lull the authorities into a complacency the situation by no means warrants, or at any rate provide them with an excuse for inaction. Again, her necessarily limited medical resources, and the old-fashioned methods allegedly used, are pointed to as detracting from her usefulness. It is perfectly true, of course, that, statistically speaking, what she achieves is little, or even negligible. But then Christianity is not a statistical view of life. That there should be more joy in heaven over one sinner who repents than over all the hosts of the just, is an anti-statistical proposition. Likewise with the work of the Missionaries of Charity. Mother Teresa is fond of saying that welfare is for a purpose – an admirable and a necessary one – whereas Christian love is for a person. The one is about numbers, the other about a man who was also God. Herein lies the essential difference between the welfare services and the service of Christ. Imagine Bernard Shaw and a mental defective on a raft that will only hold one of them. In worldly terms, the obvious course would be for Shaw to pitch the mental defective into the sea, and save himself to write more plays for the edification of mankind. Christianly speaking, jumping off and leaving the mental defective in possession of the raft would give an added glory to human life itself of greater worth than all the plays that ever have been, or will be, written. I put this point once to Sidney

Webb, a founding-father of the Welfare State, when we were walking together over Hampshire scrubland on a Sunday afternoon. It failed to register.

Again, in my television interview with Mother Teresa I raised the point as to whether, in view of the commonly held opinion that there are too many people in India, it was really worth while trying to salvage a few abandoned children who might otherwise be expected to die of neglect, malnutrition, or some related illness. It was a point, as I was to discover subsequently, so remote from her whole way of looking at life that she had difficulty in grasping it. The notion that there could in any circumstances be too many children was, to her, as inconceivable as suggesting that there are too many bluebells in the woods or stars in the sky. In the film we made in Calcutta, there is a shot of Mother Teresa holding a tiny baby girl in her hands; so minute that her very existence seemed like a miracle. As she holds this child, she says in a voice, and with an expression, of exaltation most wonderful and moving: 'See! there's life in her!' Her face is glowing and triumphant; as it might be the mother of us all glorying in what we all possess – this life in us, in our world, in the universe, which, however low it flickers or fiercely burns, is still a divine flame which no man dare presume to put out, be his motives never so humane and enlightened.

To suppose otherwise is to countenance a death-wish. Either life is always and in all circumstances sacred, or intrinsically of no account; it is inconceivable that it should be in some cases the one, and in some the other. The God Mother Teresa worships cannot, we are told, see a sparrow fall to the ground without concern. For man, made in God's image, to turn aside from this universal love, and fashion his own judgements based on his own fears and disparities, is a fearful thing, bound to have fearful consequences. What, I wonder, will posterity – assuming they are at all interested in us and our doings – make of a generation of men, who, having developed technological skills capable of producing virtually unlimited quantities of whatever they might need or desire, as well as enabling them to explore and perhaps colonize the universe, were possessed by a panic fear that soon there would not be enough food for them to eat or room for them to live? It will seem, surely, one of the most derisory, ignominious and despicable attitudes ever to be entertained in the whole of human history; though containing its own corrective. In seeking to avert an imagined calamity, the promoters and practitioners of birth-control automatically abolish themselves, leaving the future to the procreative. An interesting case of self-genocide.

I cannot pretend that, after it was over, I had a feeling that something particularly memorable had been recorded in my tele-conversation with Mother Teresa. I assumed that, as usual, the camera would have drained away whatever was real and alive in what it portrayed. The camera has a wonderful capacity for doing just this. What is more, as its definition and precision are improved, so is the process of devitalization intensified. A perfect camera would produce perfect unreality, transforming us and our human scene into a sort of universal Madame Tussaud's – something already well on the way to coming to pass. The verdict on the Mother Teresa interview was that, technically, it was barely usable, and there was for a while some doubt as to whether it was good enough for showing at all except late at night. In the end – again thanks to Oliver Hunkin – it was put out on a Sunday evening. The response was greater than I have known to any comparable programme, both in mail and in contributions of money for Mother Teresa's work. I myself received many letters enclosing cheques and money-orders ranging between a few shillings and hundreds of pounds. They came from young and old, rich and poor, educated and uneducated; all sorts and conditions of people. All of them said approximately the same thing – this woman spoke to me as no one ever has, and I feel I must help her.

Discussions are endlessly taking place about how to use a mass medium like television for Christian purposes, and all manner of devices are tried, from dialogues with learned atheists and humanists to pop versions of the psalms and psychedelic romps. Here was the answer. Just get on the screen a face shining and overflowing with Christian love; someone for whom the world is nothing and the service of Christ everything; someone reborn out of servitude to the ego and the flesh, and into the glorious liberty of the children of God. Then it doesn't matter how the face is lighted or shot; whether in front or profile, close-up or two-shot or long-shot; what questions are put, or by whom. The message comes over, as it did from St Paul – not, it would appear, particularly glib or photogenic himself. It might seem surprising, on the face of it, that an obscure nun of Albanian origins, very nervous – as was clearly apparent – in front of the camera, somewhat halting in speech, should reach English viewers on a Sunday evening as no professional Christian apologist, bishop or archbishop, moderator or

31

knockabout progressive dog-collared demonstrator ever has. But this is exactly what happened, to the surprise of all professionally concerned, including me. The message was the same message that was heard in the world for the first time two thousand years ago; as Mother Teresa showed, it has not changed its sense or lost its magic. As then, so now, it is brought, 'not with enticing words of man's wisdom, but in demonstration of the Spirit and of power; that your faith should not stand in the wisdom of men, but in the power of God'.

The Mother Teresa programme was repeated quite soon after its first showing in response to numerous requests, and the response to the repeat programme was even greater than to the original one. Altogether, something like £20,000 found its way to the Co-Workers of Mother Teresa, an organization of people, many of whom have lived in Calcutta and fallen under Mother Teresa's spell there, who exert themselves steadily and steadfastly on her behalf. No appeal for funds was made on the programme, but, of course, Mother Teresa needs money; more and more of it as her work expands. It is a matter about which she takes an extremely practical view. When the Pope visited India, on leaving he presented her with his white ceremonial motor-car. She never so much as took a ride in it, but shrewdly organized a raffle with the car as the prize, thereby raising enough money to get her leper colony started. The rich, when they come to her, are liable to leave a little less rich, which she considers is conferring a great favour on them. On the other hand, she has never accepted any government grants in connection with her medical and social work. This, she says, with another of her quizzical smiles, would involve keeping accounts. I quite see her point. The administration of her whole organization is undertaken by two nuns with one rickety typewriter between them. If auditors and that sort of thing had to be coped with, this department would need to expand, and she grudges every moment expended and penny spent other than on carrying out Christ's two commands – to love God and to love her neighbour. Actually, the efficiency with which everything is managed is quite remarkable. Computers would only spoil it.

Her own clerical work is done at night, when the Sisters have retired. She writes most of her letters in her own hand. I have a number, which I cherish. Nobody knows when she goes to sleep herself, but certainly her nights are often very abbreviated. This, of course, does not interfere with her appearance in the early morning for prayers and Mass. It is possible sometimes to see that she is tired, but not by anything in her bearing or expression or speech; just by a sort of tightness round her eyes, which still, however, look out on the world with an impregnable serenity. Does she worry? To be responsible, as she is, for houses in different parts of the world, and all the activities associated with them, as well as for an ever-growing number of Sisters at different stages in their formation, without any fixed income or source of revenue, would make most people worry. There have been times, I know, when word has come from one or other of the houses that there just was no more money left. Then you must beg, Mother Teresa might have to say. It is, I think, something she will joyously undertake herself. Begging, when it is for Christ, is a very beautiful activity, and not at all

33

demeaning. After all, the first Christians were mostly slaves. As Simone Weil says, Christianity is a religion for slaves; we have to make ourselves slaves and beggars to follow Christ. Despite this chronic financial stringency of the Missionaries of Charity, when I was instrumental in steering a few hundred pounds in Mother Teresa's direction, she astonished, and I must say enchanted, me by expending it on the chalice and ciborium for her new noviciate, 'so,' she wrote, 'you will be daily on the altar close to the Body of Christ.' Her action might, I suppose, be criticized on the same lines as the waste of spikenard ointment, but it gave me a great feeling of contentment at the time and subsequently.

After this experience of interviewing Mother Teresa, I had a consuming desire to go to Calcutta and participate in making a television programme about her and her work. This became possible in the spring of 1969, thanks to the BBC. The Corporation receives a good deal of criticism one way and another, most of it deserved. I have not been backward myself in joining in. All the same, the fact remains that it is prepared to pay for a programme such as we made in Calcutta, which no commercial network would ever undertake, especially as it offers no possibilities in the way of advertising. Rather the reverse; Mother Teresa's way of looking at life is barren soil for copy-writers, and the poorest of the poor she cherishes offer little in the way of ratings. I am duly grateful. Our producer and director was Peter Chafer, with whom I have now worked quite a lot on different sorts of programmes, always with ease and satisfaction; our cameraman, Ken Macmillan, who covered himself with glory filming the Kenneth Clark series, *Civilisation*.

Commenting to me on his work, Lord Clark said that it has a very special quality of its own because Ken is an artist. I agree.

We arrived at Calcutta airport on one of those heavy humid days for which Bengal is famous. The air seems to distil into water as one breathes it, and every movement costs one a stupendous effort – like moving dropsical limbs. A general strike, we were told, had been organized for the following day, which gave an additional feeling of suspense to an, in any case, over-charged atmosphere. As we only had five days to do our filming, we decided to go almost at once to 54A Lower Circular Road, the address of the Missionaries of Charity. Mother Teresa was waiting for us in the little courtyard of their house. The sight of her, or even the thought of her, always gives me a great feeling of happiness. This time more than ever, by way of contrast with the sombre sense of strain and anxiety all around us. Characteristically, having in the first instance resisted our coming with cameras at all, when she finally agreed, she gave us her full co-operation for the stipulated five days. She has a deep-seated and well-founded suspicion of the whole filming procedure which had to be overcome by, among other things, a charmingly persuasive letter from Cardinal Heenan, to whom she wrote in reply: 'If this TV programme is going to help people to love God better, then we will have it, but with one condition – that the Brothers and Sisters be included, as they do the work.' This condition, I may say, was faithfully observed.

The house has nothing particularly to recommend it architecturally, or in any other way. It is just a largish Calcutta house, probably occupied formerly by some prosperous vakil and his tribe of dependants. Yet the courtyard where I was to spend a good many hours during the days we were filming, has something delectable about it as I recall it; as though it were one of those courtyards in Provence with a vine climbing up the walls and spreading out to give shade, instead of just a bare stone space between walls, with the sun beating down, and, outside, the screech of the trams, the shouts, the interminable passing of bare or sandalled feet, of a Calcutta street. While Ken and the sound-recordist were setting up, Mother Teresa suggested we should go up to the chapel together. I readily agreed. The chapel is a long room with windows looking onto the street; at the end an altar, matting on the floor, and no decoration of any kind. There, too, as I have said, the noise of the street is ever-present.

We knelt side by side. I have always found praying, in any definitive sense, very difficult. Somehow the notion of putting specific requests to God strikes me as unseemly, if not absurd. I squirm when I hear trendy clergymen asking God to attend to our balance of payments, or to adjust the terms of trade more in accordance with the interests of under-developed countries, or to ensure, in a forthcoming general election, that the best man wins. Also, when old-style evangelicals, with, I am sure, utter sincerity, recount how in response to their prayers God made their businesses prosper, or brought them into contact with a particularly lucrative client. In all this field of our material well-being, individual or collective, I can never find anything to say to God except: Thy will be done. If it is true, as St Paul tells us – and it surely is – that all things work together for good to them that love God, then all that is required of us is that we should love God, and, in loving him, fall in with his purposes. Nonetheless, there is a prayer of St Augustine, a fellow communicator who once called himself, as I must, a vendor of words, that I often say over, and did on this occasion, kneeling beside Mother Teresa: 'Let me offer you in sacrifice the service of my thoughts and my tongue, but first give me what I may offer you.' I once scribbled down my own version on the flyleaf of the paperback edition of St Augustine's *Confessions:* 'Oh God, stay with me. Let no word cross my lips that is not your word, no thought enter my mind that is not your thought, no deed ever be done or entertained by me that is not your deed.' The note, I see, is dated 7 April 1968, at Salem, Oregon.

When I left Calcutta, Mother Teresa gave me a copy of the little manual of devotion she and the Sisters use. Like their hymnal, it is cyclostyled, none too efficiently. Any expenditure on printing would seem to her indefensible. In my copy, a very precious possession, she wrote:

Make us worthy, Lord, to serve our fellow men throughout the world who live and die in poverty and hunger.

Give them through our hands this day their daily bread, and by our understanding love, give peace and joy.

Words which express very simply and beautifully what she and the Sisters are about. As will be seen from the ones included in this volume, most of her prayers and meditations are in this vein. 'Love to pray,' she exhorts the Sisters, since 'prayer enlarges the heart until it is capable of containing God's gift of himself. Ask and seek, and your heart will grow big enough to receive him as your own.' At the same time, in true evangelical style, she goes to God with her needs and difficulties, and is always marvelling at the munificent response in meeting her every requirement, great and small. Those of us who cannot participate in such particular requests are not so much more sophisticated as less gifted with faith. If God cares to array the lilies of the field so splendidly, then assuredly Mother Teresa is right in believing that he cares about her and the Sisters' and Brothers' tiniest necessities in their constant endeavour to praise and serve him.

We came down from the chapel together, and the filming began. It is not just my opinion, but that of all concerned, that it proceeded with quite exceptional smoothness and speed. Our next move always seemed to be obvious; there were none of the usual breakdowns and crises. Above all, there was no bickering or quarrelling, which, in the circumstances of film-making, is almost unavoidable. In the ordinary way, making a fifty-minute documentary, which is what our film came out at, takes two to three months. To produce a sufficiency of footage in five days necessarily put a heavy strain on all concerned. The normal arrangements for time off had to be suspended; it was impossible to get a report on the film taken before moving elsewhere, so there was no chance of re-doing any that was unsatisfactory. Ken's worries in this respect were the greater because, in the burning sunshine, the camera got very hot and might have damaged the stock used. As it turned out, all was well. As far as our itinerary was concerned, in practice it was Mother Teresa who decided it. There was only one point at which a slight difference of opinion arose. It was, of course, settled in accordance with her wishes. In view of the changed arrangements, I expressed concern as to whether Mother Teresa's rickety old ambulance, in which we travelled about, needed to be sent for. Peter Chafer, wiser than I in the ways of those who walk with God, said that we should find it outside, probably with the motor turning over. So it was.

All this, as anyone with experience of filming expeditions will know, amounted to a kind of miracle. There was another actual miracle. Part of the work of the Sisters is to pick up the dying from the streets of Calcutta, and bring them into a building given to Mother Teresa for the purpose (a sometime temple dedicated to the cult of the goddess Kali), there, as she puts it, to die within sight of a loving face. Some do die; others survive and are cared for. This Home for the Dying is dimly lit by small windows high up in the walls, and Ken was adamant that filming was quite impossible there. We had only one small light with us, and to get the place adequately lighted in the time at our disposal was quite impossible. It was decided that, nonetheless, Ken should have a go, but by way of insurance he took, as well, some film in an outside court-yard where some of the inmates were sitting in the sun. In the processed film, the part taken inside was bathed in a parti-cularly beautiful soft light, whereas the part taken outside was rather dim and confused.

How to account for this? Ken has all along insisted that, technically speaking, the result is impossible. To prove the point, on his next filming expedition – to the Middle East – he used some of the same stock in a similarly poor light, with completely negative results. He offers no explanation, but just shrugs and agrees that it happened. I myself am absolutely convinced that the technically unaccountable light is, in fact, the Kindly Light Newman refers to in his well-known

41

exquisite hymn – now, as I have read, barred from up-to-date hymnals as being unduly pessimistic. Mother Teresa's Home for the Dying is overflowing with love, as one senses immediately on entering it. This love is luminous, like the haloes artists have seen and made visible round the heads of the saints. I find it not at all surprising that the luminosity should register on a photographic film. The supernatural is only an infinite projection of the natural, as the furthest horizon is an image of eternity. Jesus put mud on a blind man's eyes and made him see. It was a beautiful gesture, showing that he could bring out even in mud its innate power to heal and enrich. All the wonder and glory of mud – year by year giving creatures their food, and our eyes the delight of flowers and trees and blossoms – was crystallized to restore sight to unseeing eyes.

One thing everyone who has seen the film seems to be agreed about is that the light in the Home for the Dying is quite exceptionally lovely. This is, from every point of view, highly appropriate. Dying derelicts from the streets might normally be supposed to be somewhat repellent, giving off stenches, emitting strange groans. Actually, if the Home for the Dying were piled high with flowers and resounding with musical chants – as it may well have been in its Kali days – it could not be more restful and serene. So, the light conveys perfectly what the place is really like; an outward and visible luminosity manifesting God's inward and invisible omnipresent love. This is precisely what miracles are for – to reveal the inner reality of God's outward creation. I am personally persuaded that Ken recorded the first authentic photographic miracle.

44

It so delighted me that I fear I talked and wrote about it to the point of tedium, and sometimes of irritation. Miracles are unpopular today – to the scientifically minded because they seem to conflict with so-called scientific miracles, like bumping television programmes across the world by satellite, or going to the moon; to the ostensibly religiously minded because they remind them of miraculous claims made in the past and now discredited, which they wish to forget. Once, out at Hatch End, where Father Agnellus Andrew has his estimable set-up for instructing Roman Catholic priests and prelates in the techniques of radio and television, Peter Chafer and I showed our Mother Teresa film to a gathering of ecclesiastical brass. Afterwards, I spoke about the miracle of the light in the Home for the Dying. It troubled them, I could see. They did not want to hear about it. One or two hazarded an opinion that, no doubt, the result was due to some accidental adjustment in the camera or quality in the stock. They were happy when we moved on to other topics. In Graham Greene's brilliant satirical play, *The Potting-Shed*, he explores the theme of a free-thinking family in which a miracle occurs, and of the lengths they go to in covering up all trace of the miraculous occurrence. He can scarcely have expected to live to see the converse situation – Roman Catholics as assiduously covering up, or at any rate ignoring, a miraculous occurrence in Mother Teresa's Home for the Dying. I record the matter here in the hope that, in years to come, Christian believers may be glad to know that in a dark time the light that shone about the heads of dying derelicts brought in from the streets of Calcutta by Mother Teresa's Sisters of the Missionaries of Charity, somehow got itself recorded on film.

The next morning Mother Teresa came for us at our hotel in person in her ambulance. It was the day of the general strike, and ours was almost the only vehicle in the streets. There was an unaccustomed silence everywhere; an ominous stillness. Europeans all prudently stayed at home, as we should certainly have done were it not for Mother Teresa, who saw no reason to lose a day's work. I doubt if any other Europeans worked that day. With her, we were perfectly safe to film in the streets and walk about as we pleased. It was Peter Chafer who pointed out that, in her company, one never felt the slightest anxiety: not even over her driver's very erratic driving. He got what, in the ordinary way, would have been a hair-raising performance out of her ancient vehicle. I found Peter's attitude to Mother T, as he called her, most intriguing. He was, of course, captivated, as we all were, but I cannot say that his rather exceptionally fierce scepticism was appreciably shaken by her. On the other hand, he developed a chivalrous passion to defend her on all counts that was quite enchanting to behold. The slightest facetious or derogatory remark at her expense met with a rebuttal of exceptional ferocity which often astonished the individual concerned. She also provided him with a sort of yardstick for his work in the religious broadcasting department of the BBC. He measured other attitudes and positions which passed for being Christian, against hers, often, I fear, to find them wanting. Mother Teresa herself recognized the complete validity of Peter's position, and responded appropriately to it. On one occasion, she asked him to undertake praying for her. About his response to this request, and subsequent action, if any, he remains evasive. I may add that Mother Teresa was not at all dazzled by whatever tin-pot reputation I might have as a communicator whose words had made a certain impact here and there, and who was known accordingly. To her, Peter was the director. On one occasion – I like to think with slightly impish intent – she delivered one of her exhortations to the Sisters on the theme of how, seeing us all obey un-questioningly our director's slightest behest, so much more should the Sisters obey God's. As may be imagined, the rest of us found the theme highly diverting.

We went first to Lower Circular Road to record the Sisters' morning Mass. Because of the strike, the chapel was unaccustomedly quiet. It was, indeed, the only morning since the Missionaries of Charity took over the house that it would have been possible to record a Mass with any hope of the sound-track being usable. The priest was Father Andrew, an Australian Jesuit who had obtained special permission from his Superiors to leave the order when he was chosen by Mother Teresa to look after her male workers, the Missionary Brothers of Charity, and the boys who came into their charge. Those who have seen our film will know that he has a face of singular sweetness. I had the notion that, as there was no public or private transport, and there might easily be hostile crowds about, it would be nice if he had the ambulance to take him back. Before this could be arranged, however, he had made off by himself. From one of the chapel windows we saw him striding along the sultry, empty street, his sacerdotal equipment stuffed into an old army haversack.

Later, we visited and filmed the house where he lives with some thirty outcast boys, picked up mostly from the railway

47

station where they manage, at an age when more favoured children are at kindergarten, to live by their wits. I shall never forget his voice, when I asked him how he came to choose this particular work, and he answered: 'The need is so obvious.' It is obvious to us all, but, unlike Father Andrew, we easily manage to do little or nothing about it. Or how, when I raised the question of whether it was worth while trying to salvage some of these boys, he described the case of one of them, as he put it, a bit mental, who nonetheless, by his clowning and fooling, was of inestimable help in making newcomers to the house more at home, and so less inclined to make off. I cannot pay Father Andrew a better tribute than to say he is a perfect associate for Mother Teresa.

The day begins for the Sisters with prayers and meditation at 4.30 am, followed by Mass. After the Mass they do their washing and other chores with great vigour. Everything is done vigorously. They each have a shining bucket, which is pretty well their only possession, apart from their habits and devotional books. Then comes breakfast, after which they go off to their various outside duties – some to the Home for the Dying, some to schools and dispensaries, some to the lepers, and some to look after the unwanted babies and children who come into their charge in increasing numbers as it becomes known that, however over-worked they may be, and however over-crowded the available accommodation, none will ever be refused.

The babies come from midwives, or, as sometimes happens, are picked out of dustbins. Middle-class Indian girls and youths, emulating the civilized West, are beginning to be promiscuous, and, not having yet advanced to the point in civilization when birth-control appliances and abortions are easily available, are liable to produce unwanted children, some of them quite extraordinarily minute because their birth has been prematurely induced. These, in the Sisters' charge, soon become hearty infants. Others, at a later stage, come to the Sisters suffering from acute malnutrition, and are likewise soon restored to health. Among the lepers, in the Home for the Dying, wherever their work leads them, they bring healing and help. It is wonderful to see them going off in the morning, each loaded with a bag of bread (provided, incidentally, to their great credit, by British schoolchildren), into the city's traffic and noise; in the most literal and perfect sense, carrying out the injunction to let their light shine before men.

Their life is tough and austere by worldly standards, certainly; yet I never met such delightful, happy women, or such an atmosphere of joy as they create. Mother Teresa, as she is fond of explaining, attaches the utmost importance to this joyousness. The poor, she says, deserve not just service and dedication, but also the joy that belongs to human love. This is what the Sisters give them abundantly. Today, notoriously, the religious orders are short of vocations. Nor is the shortage being rectified by permitting nuns to use lipstick, wear mini-habits, and otherwise participate in the ways and amenities of contemporary affluence. The Missionaries of Charity, on the other hand, are multiplying at a fantastic rate. Their Calcutta house is bursting at the seams, and as each new house is opened there are volunteers clamouring to go there. As the whole story of Christendom shows, if everything is asked for, everything – and more – will be accorded; if little,

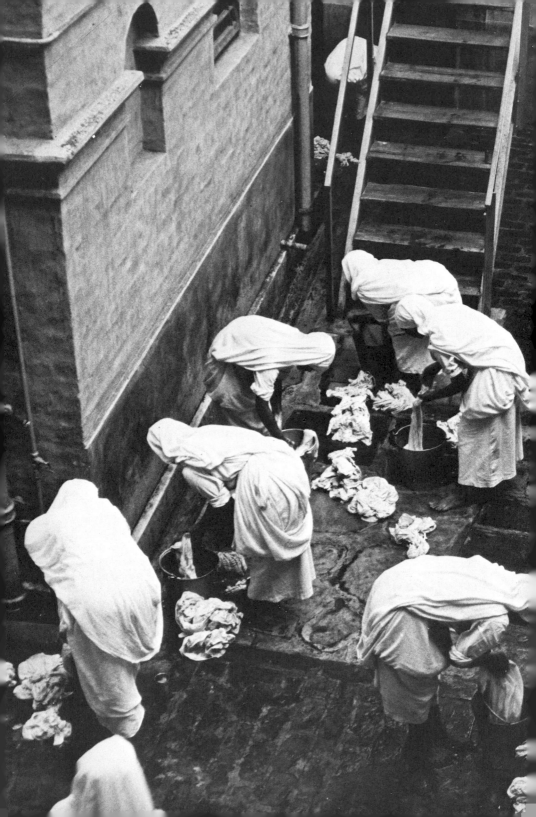

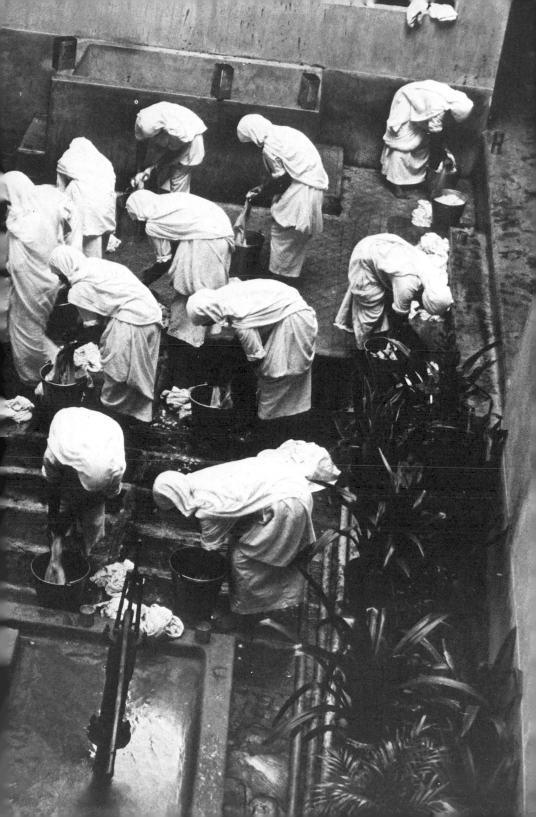

then nothing. It is curious, when this is so obvious, that nowadays the contrary proposition should seem the more accept-
able, and endeavour be directed towards softening the
austerities of the service of Christ and reducing its hazards,
with a view to attracting people into it. After all, it was in
kissing a leper's hideous sores that St Francis found the gaiety
to captivate the world and gather round him some of the most
audacious spirits of the age, to whom he offered only the glory
of being naked on the naked earth for Christ's sake. If the
demands had been less, so would the response have been. I
should never have believed it possible, knowing India as I
do over a number of years, to induce Indian girls of good
family to tend outcasts and untouchables brought in from
Calcutta streets, yet this, precisely, is the very first task that
Mother Teresa gives them to do when they come to her as
postulants. They do it, not just in obedience, but cheerfully
and ardently, and gather round her in ever greater numbers
for the privilege of doing it.

Accompanying Mother Teresa, as we did, to these different activities for the purpose of filming them – to the
Home for the Dying, to the lepers and unwanted children, I
found I went through three phases. The first was horror
mixed with pity, the second compassion pure and simple, and
the third, reaching far beyond compassion, something I had
never experienced before – an awareness that these dying
and derelict men and women, these lepers with stumps instead of hands, these unwanted children, were not pitiable,
repulsive or forlorn, but rather dear and delightful; as it
might be, friends of long standing, brothers and sisters.
How is it to be explained – the very heart and mystery of

SOMETHING BEAUTIFUL FOR GOD

the Christian faith? To soothe those battered old heads, to grasp those poor stumps, to take in one's arms those children consigned to dustbins, because it is his head, as they are his stumps and his children, of whom he said that whosoever received one such child in his name received him.

During the period of our filming I went each morning to Mass with the Sisters. One of them was always posted to let me in, and in the chapel there was a place beside Mother Teresa for me, and a missal opened at the correct page. I felt perfectly content to be worshipping with them, even though I could not, and had no wish to, partake of the Sacraments. For Mother Teresa, faith is a personal relationship with God and the incarnate Christ; the Mass the spiritual food which sustains her, without which, as she told me, she could not get through one single day or hour of the life of dedication she has chosen; the Church something she belongs to, serves and obeys as revealing and fulfilling God's purposes on earth. The various controversies and conflicts now shaking the Church scarcely touch her; they will pass, she says, and the Church will remain to perform its divinely inspired and directed function.

I know that Mother Teresa cannot understand the hesitations and doubts which make it impossible for me to accept her way of looking at the Church's present predicament, or to see it as other than an institution which a mortal hierarchy and priesthood can make or mar, sustain or let collapse. 'I don't know why,' she wrote to me, 'but very often in my heart a desire has come to be in England when you make your first Holy Communion with Jesus. I don't

53

CANISIUS COLLEGE LIBRARY
BUFFALO, N. Y.

know – but Jesus never gives desires which He does not mean to fulfil.'

On another occasion she wrote:

> *I believe the film has brought people closer to God, and so your and my hope has been fulfilled. I think now more than ever that you should use the beautiful gift God has given you for His greater glory. All that you have and all that you are and all that you can be and do – let it all be for Him and Him alone. Today what is happening in the surface of the Church will pass. For Christ, the Church is the same, today, yesterday, and tomorrow. The Apostles went through the same feeling of fear and distrust, failure and disloyalty, and yet Christ did not scold them. Just: 'Little children, little faith – why did you fear?' I wish we could love as He did – now!*

The gift she refers to so generously – far too generously – would always, such as it is, be at her and her Master's disposal. There are few things I should rather do than please her. So much so, that it almost amounts to a temptation to accept her guidance in the matter of entering the Church just because it is hers. Yet everything tells me that this would be wrong. Simone Weil found herself in a similar case vis-à-vis Father Perrin, and in a series of letters to him (included in the collection of her writings, *Waiting On God*) explained, with a cogency I could not hope to equal, the reasons that led her to decide that 'the will of God is that I should not enter the Church at present'. At the same time, she comforted herself with the thought that, 'If it is God's will that I should enter the Church, he will impose this will upon me at the exact moment when I shall have come to deserve that he should

SOMETHING BEAUTIFUL FOR GOD

so impose it.' Finally: 'I cannot help still wondering whether in these days, when so large a proportion of humanity is sunk in materialism, God does not want there to be some men and women who have given themselves to him and to Christ and who yet remain outside the Church.' I confess I have similarly wondered.

What is more difficult to convey is the longing one feels to belong to the Church; the positive envy of those the bell calls to Mass. How often I have watched them, particularly in France – those extraordinary old women in black with their lined faces, clutching their prayer-books; the children in their Sunday best, the muted fathers and the bustling mothers with wisps of black veil about their heads, all making their way to Church on a Sunday morning. What joy to be one of their number! To kneel with them, advance to the altar with them, there, side by side, swallowing the Body of Christ. Then the plainsong, the flickering candles, the solemn familiar words, the acrid incense. Of all the purposes which draw people together – excitement, cupidity, curiosity, lechery, hatred – this alone, worship, makes them seem like a loving family; abolishing the conflicts and divisions of class and race and wealth and talent, as they fall on their knees before a Father in heaven and his incarnate Son; confess their sins, renew their hopes, find the strength to snatch another mortal day from the splendid prospect opened before them of eternity, their immortal dwelling-place.

Why not, then? Because, for me, it would be fraudulent, and we cannot, dear Mother Teresa, buy faith – least of all faith – with counterfeit urges. I know perfectly well that, however much I long for it to be otherwise, the bell does not ring for me. Nor is there a place for me at the altar rail where they kneel to receive the Body of Christ. I should be an outsider there, too. The Church, after all, is an institution with a history; a past and a future. It went on crusades, it set up an inquisition, it installed scandalous popes and countenanced monstrous iniquities. Institutionally speaking, these are perfectly comprehensible, and even, in earthly terms, excusable. In the mouthpiece of God on earth, belonging, not just to history, but to everlasting truth, they are not to be defended. At least, not by me.

Today, there is the additional circumstance that the Church, for inscrutable reasons of its own, has decided to have a reformation just when the previous one – Luther's – is finally running into the sand. I make no judgement about something which, as a non-member, is no concern of mine; but if I *were* a member, then I should be forced to say that, in my opinion, if men were to be stationed at the doors of churches with whips to drive worshippers away, or inside the religious orders specifically to discourage vocations, or among the clergy to spread alarm and despondency, they could not hope to be as effective in achieving these ends as are trends and policies seemingly now dominant within the Church. Feeling so, it would be preposterous to seek admission, more particularly as, if the ecumenical course is fully run, luminaries of the Church to which I nominally belong, like the former Bishop of Woolwich, for whom – putting it mildly – I have little regard, will in due course take their place in the Roman Catholic hierarchy among the heirs of St Peter.

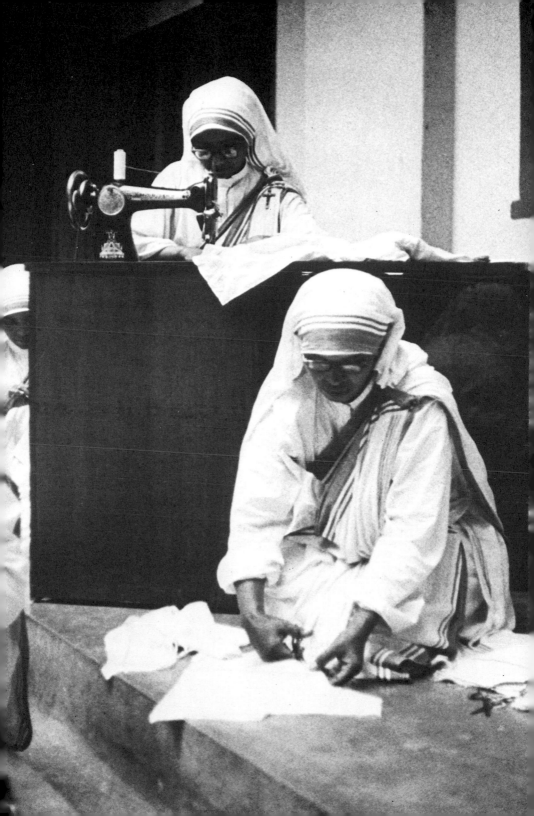

All this, I well know, would make little or no impression on Mother Teresa, whose allegiance to the Church is in quite other dimensions, deriving, as it does, from the love of God and of her neighbour enjoined on her by Christ, and the dedication to the service of the poorest of the poor that goes therewith. I can only say for myself that if ever it became clear to me that I could enter the Church in honesty and truth, I should rush to do so, the more eagerly and joyously because I should know that it would give happiness to Mother Teresa. Let me again quote Simone Weil:

> It may also be that my life will come to an end before I have felt this impulse. But one thing is absolutely certain. It is that if one day it comes about that I love God enough to deserve the grace of baptism, I shall receive this grace on that very day, infallibly, in the form which God wills, either by means of baptism in the strict sense of the word or in some other manner. In that case why should I have any anxiety? It is not my business to think about myself. My business is to think about God. It is for God to think about me.

So, in my unspoken dialogue with Mother Teresa, I conclude that I could not in honesty seek to be received into her Church; not even to please her – something that, in the ordinary way, I would go to almost any lengths to achieve. It is probable, in any case, that so potentially discontented and troublesome a member would be refused admission anyway. Mother Teresa's own loyalty is unshakable, and will survive, I am quite sure, whatever fantasies and follies may lie ahead. Her way is too clear ever to be lost; the Lord she follows too close for her ever to become separated from him. One may hear in her words and see in her life the light of the first Pentecost, which will still be shining on the last day. This is the Church's only true continuity and unity: as the old hymn puts it, its one foundation, not requiring to be re-stated or re-interpreted, nor to be re-inforced by negotiated exercises in unity. Changeless in a changing world; ever-lastingly true amidst the swirling fantasy of passing time.

Just because her faith is so sure, Mother Teresa has no need to be an evangelist in the old propagandist sense. She preaches Christ every moment of every day by living for and in him. Most contemporary Christian missionaries preface any remarks they may have to make about their work by saying that they would never dream of suggesting that Christianity is to be preferred to other religions, and look back with pitying patronage at their predecessors who took more literally the command to go and preach the gospel throughout the world. Such patronage is misplaced; one day, in a different climate of opinion, due recognition will be given to the splendid achievements in evangelism and service of Christian missionaries in India, Africa and other distant lands, by comparison with which today's tepid efforts will seem very meagre. It would be absurd to suggest that Mother Teresa is neutral as between Christianity and Hinduism. Her preference is clear for all to see and under-stand. Yet she manages nonetheless to induce high-caste Indian ladies to participate in ever increasing numbers in her work.

I look back on the days I spent with Mother Teresa in Calcutta as golden ones. Talking with her was a constant delight. She lets things out casually; as that she bought a

printing-press for the lepers so that they could print pamph-
lets and leaflets and make a little money. How, in God's name,
I asked myself, did she know what press to buy and where to
buy it? And with those stumps, how could the lepers hope to
set type? Fatuous questions! The press is there and working;
the lepers are delighted with it. She has, I found, a geography
of her own – a geography of compassion. Somehow she
hears that in Venezuela there are abandoned poor; so off the
Sisters go there, and a house is set up. Then that in Rome – in
this case, from the Pope himself – there are derelicts, as in
Calcutta. Or again, that in Australia the aboriginals and half-
castes need love and care. In each case, wherever it may be,
the call is heard and answered.

When she is away in Europe or America, she only longs
to be back in Calcutta with her poor. These are her beloved.
Walking with her among them, queuing at the dispensary,
crowding round her at the leper settlement, I kept hearing
the muttered word 'Mother!' It wasn't that they had anything to say to her or to ask her; just that they wanted to
establish contact with her, to know she was there. I quite
understood. The Sisters likewise need her presence and, when
they are stationed away from Calcutta, long for her visits.
Visiting the other houses in India, the first question always
was: 'When will she come?'

To me, Mother Teresa represents, essentially, love in
action, which is surely what Christianity is about. Perhaps, I
say to myself, the geneticists and family-planners will succeed
in constructing a broiler-house set-up where a Mother
Teresa would be unneeded and unheeded. Even then,
though, there will be some drop-outs with wounds that need

healing, wants that need satisfying, souls that need saving. There she and the Sisters will be; just as, however thickly and substantially the concrete is laid down, somewhere, somehow, there is a crack through which a tiny green shoot breaks out to remind us that this life of which we are a part is indestructible, and has its origins and its fulfilment elsewhere.

MOTHER TERESA'S
WAY OF LOVE

MOTHER TERESA'S
WAY OF LOVE

On Love of God

'Thou shalt love the Lord thy God with thy whole heart, with thy whole soul and with thy whole mind.' This is the commandment of the great God, and he cannot command the impossible. Love is a fruit in season at all times, and within reach of every hand. Anyone may gather it and no limit is set. Everyone can reach this love through meditation, spirit of prayer and sacrifice, by an intense inner life.

On Prayer

It is not possible to engage in the direct apostolate without being a soul of prayer. We must be aware of oneness with Christ, as he was aware of oneness with his Father. Our activity is truly apostolic only in so far as we permit him to work in us and through us, with his power, with his desire, with his love. We must become holy, not because we want to feel holy, but because Christ must be able to live his life fully in us. We are to be all love, all faith, all purity, for the sake of the poor we serve. And once we have learned to seek

God and his will, our contacts with the poor will become the means of great sanctity to ourselves and to others.

Love to pray – feel often during the day the need for prayer, and take trouble to pray. Prayer enlarges the heart until it is capable of containing God's gift of himself. Ask and seek, and your heart will grow big enough to receive him and keep him as your own.

On Silence

We need to find God, and he cannot be found in noise and restlessness. God is the friend of silence. See how nature – trees, flowers, grass – grow in silence; see the stars, the moon and sun, how they move in silence. Is not our mission to give God to the poor in the slums? Not a dead God, but a living, loving God. The more we receive in silent prayer, the more we can give in our active life. We need silence to be able to touch souls. The essential thing is not what we say, but what God says to us and through us. All our words will be useless unless they come from within – words which do not give the light of Christ increase the darkness.

On Holiness

Our progress in holiness depends on God and ourselves – on God's grace and on our will to be holy. We must have a real living determination to reach holiness. 'I will be a saint' means I will despoil myself of all that is not God; I will strip my

heart of all created things; I will live in poverty and detach-
ment; I will renounce my will, my inclinations, my whims
and fancies, and make myself a willing slave to the will of God.

On Humility

Let there be no pride or vanity in the work. The work is
God's work, the poor are God's poor. Put yourself completely
under the influence of Jesus, so that he may think his thoughts
in your mind, do his work through your hands, for you will
be all-powerful with him who strengthens you.

On Submission

Make sure that you let God's grace work in your souls by
accepting whatever he gives you, and giving him whatever
he takes from you.

True holiness consists in doing God's will with a smile.

On Suffering

Without our suffering, our work would just be social work,
very good and helpful, but it would not be the work of Jesus
Christ, not part of the Redemption. Jesus wanted to help by

sharing our life, our loneliness, our agony, our death. Only by being one with us he has redeemed us. We are allowed to do the same; all the desolation of the poor people, not only their material poverty, but their spiritual destitution, must be redeemed, and we must share it, for only by being one with them can we redeem them, that is, by bringing God into their lives and bringing them to God.

On Joy

Joy is prayer – Joy is strength – Joy is love – Joy is a net of love by which you can catch souls. God loves a cheerful giver. She gives most who gives with joy. The best way to show our gratitude to God and the people is to accept everything with joy. A joyful heart is the normal result of a heart burning with love. Never let anything so fill you with sorrow as to make you forget the joy of Christ Risen.

We all long for heaven where God is, but we have it in our power to be in heaven with him right now – to be happy with him at this very moment. But being happy with him now means:

> loving as he loves,
> helping as he helps,
> giving as he gives,
> serving as he serves,
> rescuing as he rescues,
> being with him twenty-four hours,
> touching him in his distressing disguise.

On Kindness

Be kind and merciful. Let no one ever come to you without coming away better and happier. Be the living expression of God's kindness: kindness in your face, kindness in your eyes, kindness in your smile, kindness in your warm greeting. In the slums we are the light of God's kindness to the poor. To children, to the poor, to all who suffer and are lonely, give always a happy smile – Give them not only your care, but also your heart.

On Our Lady

Let us ask our Lady to make our hearts 'meek and humble' as her Son's was. It is so very easy to be proud and harsh and selfish, so easy; but we have been created for greater things. How much we can learn from our Lady! She was so humble because she was all for God. She was full of grace. Tell our Lady to tell Jesus, 'They have no wine,' the wine of humility and meekness, of kindness and sweetness. She is sure to tell us, 'Do whatever he tells you.' Accept cheerfully all the chances he sends you. We learn humility through accepting humiliations cheerfully.

On Thoughtfulness

Thoughtfulness is the beginning of great sanctity. If you learn this art of being thoughtful, you will become more and

more Christ-like, for his heart was meek and he always thought of others. Our vocation, to be beautiful, must be full of thought for others. Jesus went about doing good. Our Lady did nothing else in Cana but thought of the needs of others and made their needs known to Jesus.

On Leaving Loreto

Our Lord wants me to be a free nun, covered with the poverty of the Cross. But today I learned a great lesson. The poverty of the poor must be so hard for them. When looking for a home (for a centre) I walked and walked until my legs and arms ached. I thought how much they must ache in soul and body looking for a home, food and health. Then the comfort of Loreto came to tempt me, but of my own free choice, my God, and out of love for you, I desire to remain and do whatever be your holy will in my regard. Give me courage now, this moment.

Peace*

We shall make this year a year of Peace in a particular way – to be able to do this we shall try to talk more to God and with God and less with men and to men. Let us preach the peace of Christ like he did. He went about doing good; he did not stop his works of charity because the Pharisees and others hated him or tried to spoil his Father's work. He just went about doing good. Cardinal Newman wrote: 'Help me to

* extract from a letter to the Co-Workers

spread thy fragrance everywhere I go – let me preach thee without preaching, not by words but by my example – by the catching force; the sympathetic influence of what I do, the evident fullness of the love my heart bears to thee.' Our works of love are nothing but works of peace. Let us do them with greater love and efficiency – each in her own or his own work in daily life; in your home – in your neighbour. It is always the same Christ who says:

I was hungry – not only for food, but for peace that comes from a pure heart.

I was thirsty – not for water, but for peace that satiates the passionate thirst of passion for war.

I was naked – not for clothes, but for that beautiful dignity of men and women for their bodies.

I was homeless – not for a shelter made of bricks, but for a heart that understands, that covers, that loves.

This year let us be this to Christ in our neighbour wherever the Missionaries of Charity and their Co-Workers be. Let us radiate the peace of God and so light his light and extinguish in the world and in the hearts of all men all hatred, and love for power. Let the Missionaries of Charity and the Co-Workers, in every country wherever they are, meet God with a smile – everywhere they go in everyone.

Apostle of the Unwanted

The biggest disease today is not leprosy or tuberculosis, but rather the feeling of being unwanted, uncared for and deserted by everybody. The greatest evil is the lack of love and charity, the terrible indifference towards one's neighbour who lives at the roadside assaulted by exploitation, corruption, poverty and disease.

As each one of this Society is to become a Co-Worker of Christ in the slums, each ought to understand what God and the Society expect from her. Let Christ radiate and live his life in her and through her in the slums. Let the poor seeing her be drawn to Christ and invite him to enter their homes and their lives. Let the sick and suffering find in her a real angel of comfort and consolation, let the little ones of the streets cling to her because she reminds them of him, the friend of the little ones.

Our life of poverty is as necessary as the work itself.

Only in heaven we will see how much we owe to the poor for helping us to love God better because of them.

Holy Communion

In Holy Communion we have Christ under the appearance of bread. In our work we find him under the appearance of flesh and blood. It is the same Christ. 'I was hungry, I was naked, I was sick, I was homeless.'

Daily Prayer*

JESUS MY PATIENT

Dearest Lord, may I see you today and every day in the person of your sick, and, whilst nursing them, minister unto you.

* for the Children's Home

74

Though you hide yourself behind the unattractive disguise of the irritable, the exacting, the unreasonable, may I still recognize you, and say:

'Jesus, my patient, how sweet it is to serve you.'

Lord, give me this seeing faith, then my work will never be monotonous. I will ever find joy in humouring the fancies and gratifying the wishes of all poor sufferers.

O beloved sick, how doubly dear you are to me, when you personify Christ; and what a privilege is mine to be allowed to tend you.

Sweetest Lord, make me appreciative of the dignity of my high vocation, and its many responsibilities. Never permit me to disgrace it by giving way to coldness, unkindness, or impatience.

And O God, while you are Jesus, my patient, deign also to be to me a patient Jesus, bearing with my faults, looking only to my intention, which is to love and serve you in the person of each of your sick.

Lord, increase my faith, bless my efforts and work, now and for evermore. Amen.

Go Tell Everyone

God's Spirit is in my heart,
He has called me and set me apart,
This is what I have to do,
What I have to do.

He's sent me to give the good news to the poor,
Tell prisoners that they are prisoners no more,
Tell blind people that they can see,
And set the down-trodden free,
And go tell everyone the news that the kingdom of God has come,
And go tell everyone the news that God's kingdom has come.

Just as the Father sent me,
So I'm sending you out to be
My witnesses throughout the world,
The whole of the world.

Don't carry a load in your pack,
You don't need two shirts on your back,
The workman can earn his own keep,
Can earn his own keep.

Don't worry what you have to say,
Don't worry because on that day,
God's Spirit will speak in your heart,
Will speak in your heart.

Whatsoever You Do

When I was hungry, you gave me to eat,
When I was thirsty, you gave me to drink,

Whatsoever you do to the least of my brothers,
that you do unto me.
Now enter the house of my Father.

When I was homeless, you opened your doors,
When I was naked, you gave me your coat,

When I was weary, you helped me find rest,
When I was anxious, you calmed all my fears,

When I was little, you taught me to read,
When I was lonely, you gave me your love,

When in a prison, you came to my cell,
When on a sick bed, you cared for my needs,

In a strange country, you made me at home,
Seeking employment, you found me a job,

Hurt in a battle, you bound up my wounds,
Searching for kindness, you held out your hand,

When I was Negro, or Chinese, or White,
Mocked and insulted you carried my cross,

When I was aged, you bothered to smile,
When I was restless, you listened and cared,

You saw me covered with spittle and blood,
You knew my features, though grimy with sweat,

When I was laughed at, you stood by my side,
When I was happy, you shared in my joy.

MOTHER TERESA
SPEAKS

MOTHER TERESA
SPEAKS

MALCOLM

Mother Teresa, when did all this begin with you? I don't
mean just your house here. But when did the feeling that you
must dedicate yourself to poor people come to you?

MOTHER TERESA

It was many years ago when I was at home with my people.

MALCOLM

Where was that?

MOTHER TERESA

In Skopje in Yugoslavia. I was only twelve years old then.
I lived at home and with my parents; we children used to
go to a non-Catholic school but we also had very good
priests who were helping the boys and the girls to follow
their vocation according to the call of God. It was then that
I first knew I had a vocation to the poor.

MALCOLM

That was when it all started.

MOTHER TERESA

Yes, in 1922.

MALCOLM

It was then you decided your life was not to be one of pleasing yourself, but was to be given to God in a very special way.

MOTHER TERESA

I wanted to be a missionary, I wanted to go out and give the life of Christ to the people in the missionary countries. At that time some missionaries had gone to India from Yugoslavia. They told me the Loreto nuns were doing work in Calcutta and other places. I offered myself to go out to the Bengal Mission, and from there they sent me to India in 1929.

MALCOLM

When did you take your final vows?

MOTHER TERESA

I took the first vows in Loreto in 1931. Then in 1937 I took final vows in Loreto.

MALCOLM

Between the age of twelve and taking your final vows did you have any doubts, any hesitations about taking on this very difficult way of life?

MOTHER TERESA

At the beginning, between twelve and eighteen I didn't want to become a nun. We were a very happy family. But when I was eighteen, I decided to leave my home and become a nun, and since then, this forty years, I've never doubted even for a second that I've done the right thing; it was the will of God. It was his choice.

84

MALCOLM

And this has given you complete peace and happiness.

MOTHER TERESA

The happiness that no one can take from me. And there has never been a doubt or any unhappiness.

MALCOLM

When you were in Loreto you were teaching. Did you like teaching?

MOTHER TERESA

I love teaching most of all. At Loreto I was in charge of a school in the Bengali department. At that time most of the girls that are now with me were girls in school. I was teaching them.

MALCOLM

And all this came to an end when you became aware of certain circumstances in the world outside.

MOTHER TERESA

It was a call within my vocation. It was a second calling. It was a vocation to give up even Loreto where I was very happy and to go out in the streets to serve the poorest of the poor.

MALCOLM

Mother, how did it happen, the second vocation?

MOTHER TERESA

In 1946 I was going to Darjeeling, to make my retreat. It was in that train, I heard the call to give up all and follow him into the slums to serve him among the poorest of the poor.

MALCOLM

So you took the decision – at least, in a way, it was taken for you but you accepted what the inner voice asked of you.

MOTHER TERESA

I knew it was his will, and that I had to follow him. There was no doubt that it was going to be his work. But I waited for the decision of the Church.

MALCOLM

You had to get permission from the ecclesiastical authorities to come out of the Loreto convent; how long did that take?

MOTHER TERESA

I had first to apply to the Archbishop of Calcutta. Then with his approval the Mother General of the Loreto nuns gave me permission to write to Rome. I had to do this because I was a nun who had taken final vows and nuns cannot be allowed to leave the convent. I wrote to the Holy Father, Pope Pius XII, and by return post I got the answer on the 12th of April. He said that I could go out and be an unenclosed nun. That means to live the life of a religious, but under obedience to the Archbishop of Calcutta.

MALCOLM

How many years ago was that?

MOTHER TERESA

That was in 1948.

MALCOLM

In your letter to the Pope what did you say you wanted to do?

MOTHER TERESA

I told him that I had a vocation, that God was calling me to give up all and to surrender myself to him in the service of the poorest of the poor in the slums.

MALCOLM

I have seen your Loreto convent and it is lovely. It must have been hard to walk out of that beautiful garden, out of that quiet peaceful place into these terrible noisy streets.

MOTHER TERESA

That was the sacrifice.

MALCOLM

What did you do then?

MOTHER TERESA

I left the Loreto convent and I went first to the Sisters in Patna to get a little training in medical work so that I could enter the houses of the poor; up till then I was only a teacher and I could not start on work with teaching. First I had to go into the homes and see the children and the sick. At the first little school I started on the first day there were five children. Slowly after that we had more and more children. At present in that place we have got over five hundred children who come daily to school.

MALCOLM

In the place where you started?

MOTHER TERESA

Yes, where I started, out in the compound of a family in the slums.

SOMETHING BEAUTIFUL FOR GOD

MALCOLM

When I think of Calcutta and of the appallingness of so much of it, it seems extraordinary that one person could just walk out and decide to tackle this thing.

MOTHER TERESA

I was so sure then, and I'm still convinced, that it is he and not I. That's why I was not afraid; I knew that if the work was mine it would die with me. But I knew it was his work, that it will live and bring much good.

MALCOLM

You presumably just taught kids off the streets. What did you teach them?

MOTHER TERESA

I began with teaching them their alphabet because, though they were all big children, they had never been to school and no school wanted them. Then we had practical lessons on hygiene; told them how to wash themselves. Next day two or three girls came from the school where I had taught, they helped me with the children. Gradually the work started to grow and some ladies from Calcutta who had been teachers in the school where I had been teaching also came. And so the work started growing.

MALCOLM

I suppose you must have had some money; where did that come from?

MOTHER TERESA

At first I had only five rupees, but gradually, as people came to know what I was doing, they brought things and money.

It was all divine providence because right from the very first I didn't ask for money.

MALCOLM

The money had to be voluntary contributions.

MOTHER TERESA

It was all a gift. I wanted to serve the poor purely for the love of God. I wanted to give the poor what the rich get with money.

MALCOLM

You've got your school going, and it's growing; you've got a few helpers, and you've got a bit of money and gifts coming in. What happened then?

MOTHER TERESA

The Sisters started coming in 1949; the first Sister who joined our congregation was Sister Agnes. She is my assistant now.

MALCOLM

She was a schoolgirl in Loreto, wasn't she?

MOTHER TERESA

Yes, and the first ten girls who came were all students that I had taught in the school. One by one, they surrendered themselves to God to serve the poorest of the poor. They wanted to give their all to God. Then other helpers came; doctors and nurses came on a voluntary basis to help us. In 1952 we opened the first Home for the Dying.

MALCOLM

When you say Home for the Dying, you mean that these are
people on the streets who have been abandoned and are
dying.

MOTHER TERESA

Yes, the first woman I saw I myself picked up from the street.
She had been half eaten by the rats and ants. I took her to the
hospital but they could not do anything for her. They only
took her in because I refused to move until they accepted her.
From there I went to the municipality and I asked them to give
me a place where I could bring these people because on the
same day I had found other people dying in the streets. The
health officer of the municipality took me to the temple, the
Kali Temple, and showed me the dormashalah where the
people used to rest after they had done their worship of Kali
goddess. It was an empty building; he asked me if I would
accept it. I was very happy to have that place for many
reasons, but especially knowing that it was a centre of worship
and devotion of the Hindus. Within twenty-four hours we
had our patients there and we started the work of the home
for the sick and dying who are destitutes. Since then we have
picked up over twenty-three thousand people from the streets
of Calcutta of which about fifty per cent have died.

MALCOLM

What exactly are you doing for these dying people? I know
you bring them in to die there. What is it you are doing for
them or seeking to do for them?

MOTHER TERESA

First of all we want to make them feel that they are wanted, we want them to know that there are people who really love them, who really want them, at least for the few hours that they have to live, to know human and divine love. That they too may know that they are the children of God, and that they are not forgotten and that they are loved and cared about and there are young lives ready to give themselves in their service.

MALCOLM

What happens to the ones who don't die?

MOTHER TERESA

Those who are able to work we try to find some work for them, the others we try to send them to homes where they can spend at least a few years in happiness and comfort.

MALCOLM

Who brings them to you, Mother? I mean who, as it were, delivers them to you?

MOTHER TERESA

At the beginning the Sisters used to find them in the streets and pick them up.

MALCOLM

As you did this first woman.

MOTHER TERESA

Yes. But as the work became more and more known, more and more people came to hear that there was a place where these people could be cared for. They telephone for the municipal ambulance and it comes and picks them up and brings them to us. But under one condition, that they have first to take them to the nearest hospital.

MALCOLM

You only want people who cannot get in anywhere else; for whom this is the last refuge, is that right?

MOTHER TERESA

Yes, the home is meant only for the street cases and cases that no hospital wants or for people who have absolutely no one to take care of them.

MALCOLM

As this work developed from the school to looking after sick people, you needed more and more hands to help. Did they come along?

MOTHER TERESA

God has been very wonderful to us because as the work kept growing, our vocations also kept growing. In 1950 in October, the Holy Father made our little community into a diocesan congregation. Fifteen years later he raised it to a pontifical congregation; that means that we are now directly under the Holy Father. This has been the biggest miracle of all because as a rule congregations are not raised to the pontifical order so fast. It takes most of them many years, thirty, forty years sometimes, before they become a pontifical. This shows the great love and appreciation the Holy Father has for our work and for the congregation.

MALCOLM

What did the numbers of your Sisters go up to in the first few years?

MOTHER TERESA

When the congregation became a diocesan congregation we

were only twelve; that was in 1950. Gradually the numbers kept on increasing. For ten years we did not move out of Calcutta, because we had to train our Sisters for the work. In 1959 when we opened the first house in Dranchi and then one in Delhi, the numbers of Sisters started increasing and we began getting girls from the very places where we had opened houses.

MALCOLM

What sort of girls were they for the most part?

MOTHER TERESA

Mostly middle-class, but some were of the richer and higher class. There were quite a number of Anglo-Indian girls who joined the congregation at that time.

MALCOLM

Educated girls.

MOTHER TERESA

Very well educated most of them.

MALCOLM

Wasn't it a rather terrible experience for educated girls, from middle-class or upper-class homes, suddenly to be mixing with the poorest, the most wretched and most ill from the streets?

MOTHER TERESA

These girls wanted to give their best, because in our society we have to make a total surrender to God; this is the spirit of the community. They wanted to achieve this fulfilment in their own lives by giving all to God, giving up their position,

96

their home, their future and dedicating all of it wholly to the poorest of the poor. They thought they couldn't give enough to God who had given them this beautiful vocation of serving the poorest of the poor.

MALCOLM

How do they find the strength to give this?

MOTHER TERESA

From the day they join the community we spend a very good deal of time in training the Sisters, especially in the spirit and the life of the society which is beautifully defined in the constitution. This is the written will of God for us. Also, side by side with the spiritual training, they have to go to the slums. Slum work and this meeting with the people is a part of the noviciate training. This is something special to us as a congregation because as a rule novices do not go out, but to be able to understand the meaning of our fourth vow, which promises that we give our whole hearted free service to the poorest of the poor – to Christ in his distressing disguise. Because of this it is necessary that they came face to face with the reality, so as to be able to understand what their life is going to be, when they will have taken their vows and when they will have to meet Christ twenty-four hours a day in the poorest of the poor in the slums.

MALCOLM

Did many find it too much, Mother?

MOTHER TERESA

Very few, very, very few have left. We can count them on our fingers. It's the most extraordinary thing that so many of our Sisters have been so faithful right from the very first.

97

MALCOLM

Although it was such a severe test, they found fulfilment in it.

MOTHER TERESA

It was a challenge for them. They wanted to give everything, and they wanted the hardest. We have to live this life, this hard life, to be able to continue the work among the people. The work is only the expression of the love we have for God. We have to pour our love on someone. And the people are the means of expressing our love for God.

MALCOLM

Spending a few days with you, I have been immensely struck by the joyfulness of these Sisters who do what an outsider might think to be almost impossibly difficult and painful tasks.

MOTHER TERESA

That's the spirit of our society, that total surrender, loving trust and cheerfulness. We must be able to radiate the joy of Christ, express it in our actions. If our actions are just useful actions that give no joy to the people, our poor people would never be able to rise up to the call which we want them to hear, the call to come closer to God. We want to make them feel that they are loved. If we went to them with a sad face, we would only make them much more depressed.

MALCOLM

Even though you took them things they needed.

MOTHER TERESA

It is not very often things they need. What they need much more is what we offer them. In these twenty years of work amongst the people, I have come more and more to realize that it is being unwanted that is the worst disease that any human being can ever experience. Nowadays we have found medicine for leprosy and lepers can be cured. There's medicine for TB and consumptives can be cured. For all kinds of diseases there are medicines and cures. But for being unwanted, except there are willing hands to serve and there's a loving heart to love, I don't think this terrible disease can ever be cured.

MALCOLM
And that is the disease you're looking after?

MOTHER TERESA
This is what we are aiming at, to bring to the people the willing hands to serve and the hearts to go on loving them, and to look at them as Christ.

MALCOLM
Besides the sick people, you've got a lot of children, haven't you?

MOTHER TERESA
Yes.

MALCOLM
Where do they come from?

MOTHER TERESA
Many of those children are unwanted by their parents; some we pick up, some we get from hospitals: they have been left there by their parents. Some we bring from the jail, some are brought to us by the police. By whatever means they are brought to us, up to now we have never refused a child.

MALCOLM

Somehow you fit them in, however many may come?

MOTHER TERESA

We always have one more bed for one more child.

MALCOLM

So you've never had to turn one down?

MOTHER TERESA

No.

MALCOLM

Some people say that there are too many children in India, and yet you're saving children many of whom would otherwise die.

MOTHER TERESA

Yes, many would die, especially among those children that are unwanted. Quite possibly they would have been either thrown away or killed. But that way is not for us; our way is to preserve life, the life of Christ in the life of the child.

MALCOLM

So you wouldn't agree with people who say there are too many children in India.

MOTHER TERESA

I do not agree because God always provides. He provides for the flowers and the birds, for everything in the world that he has created. And those little children are his life. There can never be enough.

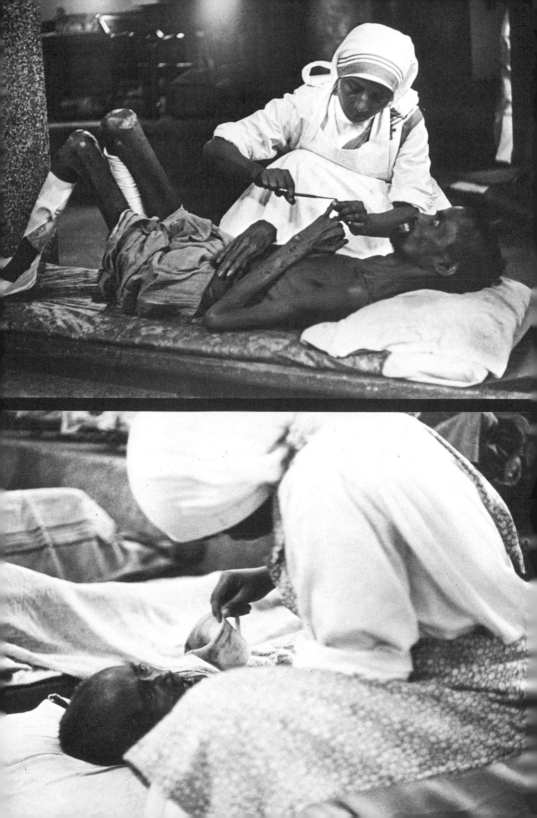

MALCOLM

Then what about the lepers? How did your work for them begin, Mother?

MOTHER TERESA

In 1957 we started with five lepers who came to our home because they had been thrown out from their work. They could get no shelter, they had to go begging. With them a doctor soon came to help us and he's still with us, Dr Senn. He has also been training our Sisters for the leprosy work, because he's a specialist in leprosy work. Among the lepers there are many well-educated people, many rich and capable people. But owing to the disease, they have been thrown out of society, out of their homes, by their relations, and very often even their own children do not want to see them any more. They get isolated from their own families and have no alternative but to turn to begging. Very often you see people coming up to Bengal from the south and the Bengal people going to the furthest north just to be far away from the people and from the places where they have been known and served and loved. We have among our lepers here in Calcutta very capable people who have had very high positions in life. But owing to the disease, they are now living in the slums, unknown, unloved and uncared for. Thank God our Sisters are there to love them and to be their friends and to bring the rich closer to them.

MALCOLM

This is a terrible disease and there are many lepers. What can – what can the Sisters do for them?

MOTHER TERESA

Most of our Sisters have been specially trained for the leprosy work. And with the new drugs that we are getting from the States and from England, we are able to stop the disease if the people come in time. That's why, though we have so many in Calcutta – we have nearly ten thousand people that are under our care – still we are very happy because that's a sign that the lepers are beginning to know about this disease and to want to be healed. If they come at once, as soon as they realize that they have got a patch of leprosy on their body, they have every opportunity in two years' time to be completely cured.

MALCOLM

And what about the ones that are past curing?

MOTHER TERESA

We are trying to build a town of peace on the land that Government gave us some years back, thirty-four acres of land. This place is called Shanti Nagar. We are building a rehabilitation centre there so that those lepers who have been healed can be trained for ordinary works and be able to have small industries in their own homes and so be able to live an ordinary citizen's life when they come back to their places. Then they won't have to go round and beg.

MALCOLM

Your community is growing and spreading, is this going to go on; are you going to spread all over the world?

MOTHER TERESA

At present we are in twenty-five cities in India, and outside of

India we are in Ceylon and Tanzania, in Venezuela and in Rome. As long as God gives me vocations, it's a sign that God wants us to spread, and wherever there are poor we shall go and serve them.

MALCOLM

So the process is likely to continue?

MOTHER TERESA

Well, if he gives vocations it's a sign that he wants us to go out to the poor.

MALCOLM

He's given you a good lot, hasn't he?

MOTHER TERESA

Yes. Thank God this year has been an extraordinary year, and we are expecting many more to join us in June and also next January.

MALCOLM

A girl hears of your work amongst the very poor and feels this to be her vocation. What happens next?

MOTHER TERESA

When these girls come, they join the aspirants. They spend about six months in seeing our work. They have to see if this is what God wants for them. And we have to see if they really have a vocation for this kind of life and work. At the same time they have to learn English because that is the language of our community, and as we do not have enough spiritual books in Indian languages we have to use English books. Also, in India we have so many languages, and the Sisters come from all over India, so it would be very difficult to train them in spiritual life if there are so many languages being used in one community; so because of all this we have accepted to use English. After that they have to spend six months in postulancy where they begin to learn the rudiments of spiritual life. After these six months they join the noviciate for two years. During that time they have an intensive spiritual training in theology, Church history and the Scriptures, and especially in the rules and the constitution of our community. Because the Sisters are going to bind themselves by vows, they must know exactly what these vows are going to mean to them. The vow of poverty is very, very strict in our congregation because to be able to love the poor and to know the poor we must be poor ourselves. We take the vow of chastity, of giving our hearts complete and undivided to Christ – an entire dedication to Christ. We have also the vow of obedience and we take all the other vows according to obedience. We have to do God's will in everything. We also take a special vow which other congregations don't take, that of giving whole hearted free service to the poor. This vow means that we cannot work for the rich; neither can we accept any money for the work we do. Ours has to be a free service, and to the poor.

MALCOLM
That is asking a lot, isn't it? You ask these girls to live like the poorest of the poor, to devote all their time and energy and life to the service of the poor.

MOTHER TERESA
That is what they want to give. They want to give to God

everything. They know very well that it's to Christ the hungry and Christ the naked and Christ the homeless that they are doing it. And this conviction and this love is what makes the giving a joy. That's why you see the Sisters are very happy. They are not forced to be happy; they are naturally happy because they feel that they have found what they have looked for.

MALCOLM

But one thing that would strike, I think, anybody looking on is the magnitude of what you're tackling and, apart from your own extraordinary faith and the marvellous faith of your Sisters, the smallness of your resources. Don't you ever feel discouraged? Some people believe that these things should be done by great state organizations, they feel that a few loving souls trying to tackle such a thing is absurd. What do you think about all that?

MOTHER TERESA

If the work is looked at just by our own eyes and only from our own way, naturally, we ourselves we can do nothing. But in Christ we can do all things. That's why this work has become possible, because we are convinced that it is he, he who is working with us and through us in the poor and for the poor.

MALCOLM

The stimulus, the fire, the strength of what you're doing comes from that?

MOTHER TERESA

It comes from Christ and the Sacrament.

MALCOLM

Which is why you begin each day with Mass?

MOTHER TERESA

Yes. Without him we could do nothing. And it is there at the altar that we meet our suffering poor. And in him that we see that suffering can become a means to greater love, and greater generosity.

*   *   *

MALCOLM

Sister Joseph, when did you take your final vows?

SISTER JOSEPH

I took my final vows in 1964 on the 14th of April.

MALCOLM

That's five years ago. It's a terrific step to take, isn't it? Many people would think it's an absolutely lunatic step. You leave a world full of interesting things and exciting things and you come to this austere life which is the life of the poor. You adopt the standard of life of the poor, and you spend all your time with the poorest and lowliest people. Isn't this rather a mad thing to do?

SISTER JOSEPH

That is precisely why I came here; I came because I wanted a very hard life. I wanted to be able to give up something.

MALCOLM

And has it made you happy?

SISTER JOSEPH

Happy? Very happy. Because I feel I can give so much to help others.

MALCOLM

But this business of spending your time with people who are dying, with lepers, with unwanted children. The other day I saw you with these people and they were all clamouring for help. Doesn't it make you sometimes want a different sort of life?

SISTER JOSEPH

No. I am sometimes dead tired, but dead tired, and also very very happy that I've been able to do something for someone else.

MALCOLM

Why this sort of life?

SISTER JOSEPH

I had heard about the hardships of this congregation, and I felt that I wanted to give so much to God and that's why I particularly came here. It was a challenge to me.

MALCOLM

How old were you?

SISTER JOSEPH

I was twenty-four when I came here.

MALCOLM

So you knew all about the world?

SOMETHING BEAUTIFUL FOR GOD

SISTER JOSEPH

Yes, I knew. I had been working in an office for eight years, also I was a music teacher. And I have no regrets.

MALCOLM

Your life here is a fulfilment and it brings you happiness.

SISTER JOSEPH

Absolutely. Not a day's regret, not a moment of regret.

MALCOLM

Although it has deprived you of the only things which, particularly in this age, people think make life worth living.

SISTER JOSEPH

I think happiness for me is that I'm able to help others, and be with others; of course there are many things that we miss.

MALCOLM

Such as?

SISTER JOSEPH

Music. I love to play the piano. Now I don't. But I'm happy I was able to give up something.

MALCOLM

But you can sing, I've heard you.

SISTER JOSEPH

I try.

MALCOLM

You sing very beautifully.

SISTER JOSEPH

I try.

*   *   *

MALCOLM

Mother Teresa, after I met you in London, the only thing I wanted to do was to come and see you and your work here and now I've seen it. It's a shining light. But behind the work, which is wonderful and needed, as you keep saying and I'm sure you're right, there's something else, which is your faith. Tell me about that because I think you will agree with me it's something that's rather lacking in the world today.

MOTHER TERESA

Faith is a gift of God. Without it there would be no life. And our work, to be fruitful and to be all for God, and beautiful, has to be built on faith. Faith in Christ who has said, 'I was hungry, I was naked, I was sick, and I was homeless and you did that to me.' On these words of his all our work is based.

MALCOLM

How are people to have this faith that is lacking in the world today?

MOTHER TERESA

It is lacking because there is so much selfishness and so much gain only for self. But faith to be true has to be a giving love. Love and faith go together. They complete each other.

MALCOLM

How are people to find this? Our fellow men, or many of them, perhaps including myself, have lost their way. You have found the way. How do you help them to find the way?

MOTHER TERESA

By getting them in touch with the people, for in the people they will find God.

MALCOLM

You mean that the road to faith and the road to God is via our fellow human beings?

MOTHER TERESA

Because we cannot see Christ we cannot express our love to him; but our neighbours we can always see, and we can do to them what if we saw him we would like to do to Christ.

MALCOLM

You don't think there's a danger that people might mistake the means for the end, and feel that serving their fellow men was an end in itself. Do you think there's a danger of that?

MOTHER TERESA

There is always the danger that we may become only social workers or just do the work for the sake of the work.

MALCOLM

That's what I was thinking of. Isn't it a danger?

MOTHER TERESA

It is a danger; if we forget to whom we are doing it. Our works are only an expression of our love for Christ. Our hearts need to be full of love for him and since we have to express that love in action, naturally then the poorest of the poor are the means of expressing our love for God.

MALCOLM

I understand that, and even in this short visit I've sensed it as I never have before. These lepers and these little children that you get off the street, they're not just destitute people, to be pitied, but marvellous people. Anyone who's well can pity a man who's sick. Anyone who has enough can pity someone who hasn't enough. But I think what you do is to make one see that these people are not just to be pitied; they are marvellous people. How do you do this?

MOTHER TERESA

That's just what a Hindu gentleman said: that they and we are doing social work, and the difference between them and us is that they were doing it for something and we were doing it to somebody. This is where the respect and the love and the devotion come in, that we give it and we do it to God, to Christ, and that's why we try to do it as beautifully as possible. Because it is a continual contact with Christ in his work, it is the same contact we have during Mass and in the Blessed Sacrament. There we have Jesus in the appearance of bread. But here in the slums, in the broken body, in the children, we see Christ and we touch him.

MALCOLM

Beautiful is almost your favourite word, isn't it? You were saying, even when we asked you to do this programme – and I know you were very reluctant to do it – Well, let's do something beautiful for God! But what I want to say is how do you – how do we – how can you make other people see this, that it's not just to pity, it's not just to meet physical needs, material needs which are desperate and should be met, but that there's something more that gives it its reality?

MOTHER TERESA

In our work we have many people whom we call Co-Workers, and I want them to give their hands to serve the people and their hearts to love the people. For, unless they come in very close contact with them, it is very difficult for them to know who the poor are. That's why here in Calcutta especially we have many non-Christians and Christians working together at the Home for the Dying and other places. We have groups who are preparing the bandages and medicine for the lepers. For example an Australian came some time ago, and he said that he wanted to give a big donation. But after giving the donation, he said, 'That is something outside of me, but I want to give something of me.' And now he comes regularly to the Home for the Dying, and he shaves the people and talks to them. He could have spent that time on himself, not just his money. He wanted to give something of himself and he gives it.

MALCOLM

In other words this other part is really in a way a greater gift.

MOTHER TERESA

It is the harder part.

MALCOLM

The harder part. But you of course influenced him to do that; he sees you, and everybody who sees you or talks to you would to some extent feel like he does. But I am thinking of the Western world where I live and which you sometimes visit. This world also is in a different way a very unhappy place, Mother. There are rich people there who have surplus wealth and kindly impulses. What they lack is this spark, this personal feeling, which faith gives and which could suddenly make it possible for them to do all the things that should be done. How would you take that faith to them?

115

MOTHER TERESA

By doing work with them. I always insist on people doing
the work with us, and for us, and for the people. I never speak
to them of money or ask for things from them. I just ask them
to come and love the people, to give their hands to serve them
and their hearts to love them. And when they come in touch
with them, then their first impulse is to do something for
them. And next time they come, they're already involved.
When they have been for some time in Calcutta or in any
other place, they feel that they are part of the people. Once
they have realized how lovable these people are, just how they
are and how much they can give to them.

MALCOLM

Shouldn't the churches be influencing people in the West in
this way, perhaps more than they are?

MOTHER TERESA

I do not know so much the situation in the West because I
have been away for such a long time – forty years. But now
more and more there's this Lenten raising of money to help
the poorest. It's growing, and people are beginning to be more
and more conscious that there are in the world people who
are hungry and who are naked, and who are sick and who
have no shelter. And the rich want to share the hardship in
some way just a little bit sometimes; the difficulty is that they
don't give until it hurts. The new generation, especially the
children, are understanding better. The children in England
are making sacrifices to give a slice of bread to our children,
and the children of Denmark are making sacrifices to give a
glass of milk to our children daily, and the children of

117

Germany are making sacrifices to give one multi-vitamin daily to a child. These are the ways to greater love. These children when they grow up, they will have faith and love and a desire to serve and to give more.

MALCOLM

Would you agree that one of the troubles is that twentieth-century man always thinks there must be some collective solution. He would say, there is Mother Teresa, she saves so many people, she helps so many people, she saves so many children. But this is just a fleabite; this is nothing; there must be some other way of doing it. And his feeling about this makes him less inclined to throw himself in the way that you want into the sort of work that you're doing.

MOTHER TERESA

I do not agree with the big way of doing things. To us what matters is an individual. To get to love the person we must come in close contact with him. If we wait till we get the numbers, then we will be lost in the numbers. And we will never be able to show that love and respect for the person. I believe in person to person; every person is Christ for me, and since there is only one Jesus, that person is only one person in the world for me at that moment.

MALCOLM

I'm sure that's right, but the difficulty that I see is how to make these people whose minds had been formed in the circumstances of today realize this. Even the churches, who should understand this since it is the gospel on which they're based, fail to inculcate this particular feeling of person to person.

118

MOTHER TERESA

I believe the people of today do not think that the poor are like them as human beings. They look down on them. But if they had that deep respect for the dignity of poor people, I am sure it would be – it would be easy for them to come closer to them, and to see that they, too, are the children of God, and that they have as much right to the things of life and of love and of service as anybody else. In these times of development everybody is in a hurry and everybody's in a rush, and on the way there are people falling down, who are not able to compete. These are the ones we want to love and serve and take care of.

MALCOLM

And do with them beautiful things for God.

MOTHER TERESA

We ourselves feel that what we are doing is just a drop in the ocean. But if that drop was not in the ocean I think the ocean will be less because of that missing drop. For example, if we didn't have our schools in the slums – they are nothing, they are just little primary schools where we teach the children to love the school and to be clean and so on – if we didn't have these little schools, those children, those thousands of children, would be left in the streets. So we have to choose either to take them and give them just a little, or leave them in the street. It is the same thing for our Home for the Dying and our home for the children. If we didn't have that home, those people we have picked up, they would have died in the street. I think it was worth while having that home even for those few people to die beautifully, with God and in peace.

MALCOLM

I agree with you. To me one of the most wonderful things about your work is that you make one see that these poor people are wonderful people, that these children are exquisite children, this and the fact that you have the principle that no one must ever be refused. That there is no qualification, no selectivity. You have now got Brothers also, haven't you? How did that come about, Mother?

MOTHER TERESA

In 1963 the Archbishop gave me permission to start the Brothers. We felt a need for men who would take care of the boys in the school and the men in the Home for the Dying. And there are other things that we as women cannot do for the men in the docks and so on. His Grace gave the permission and now for the last two years their congregation is a diocesan congregation. Father Andrew who was a Jesuit got permission from the Holy Father to join the Brothers. And he's their Superior now, he takes care of them.

MALCOLM

How many of them are there, Mother?

MOTHER TERESA

At present there are ninety-two.

MALCOLM

And they go and pick people up and so on?

MOTHER TERESA

They do exactly the same kind of work and they live the same life as we do.

MALCOLM

But specialize in those parts that are more appropriate for a man than a woman?

MOTHER TERESA

Yes. They also work for the women in the slums, but much more for the boys and for the crippled men.

MALCOLM

So they too have been roped in to doing something beautiful for God.

A DOOR OF
UTTERANCE

A DOOR OF
UTTERANCE

When the various difficulties in the way of making our film about Mother Teresa and the Missionaries of Charity had all been dealt with, and we were in a position to go ahead, Mother Teresa wrote to me: 'Now let us do something beautiful for God.' I found the phrase enchanting, with a sparkle and gaiety very characteristic of her. It continued to echo in my mind, and when the time came to choose a title for the film, *Something Beautiful for God* seemed the obvious one. Likewise for this book.

Doing something beautiful for God is, for Mother Teresa, what life is about. Everything, in that it is for God, becomes beautiful, whatever it may be; as does every human soul participating in this purpose, whoever he or she may be. In manifesting this, in themselves and in their lives and work, Mother Teresa and the Missionaries of Charity provide a living witness to the power and truth of what Jesus came to proclaim. His light shines in them. When I think of them in Calcutta, as I often do, it is not the bare house in a dark slum that is conjured up in my mind, but a light shining and a joy abounding. I see them diligently and cheerfully constructing something beautiful for God out of the human misery and affliction that lies around them. One of their leper settlements is near a slaughter-house whose stench in the ordinary way might easily make me retch. There, with Mother Teresa, I scarcely noticed it; another fragrance had swallowed it up.

For those of us who find difficulty in grasping with our minds Christ's great propositions of love which make such dedication possible, someone like Mother Teresa is a godsend. She is this love in person; through her, we can reach it, and hold it, and incorporate it in ourselves. Everyone feels this. I was watching recently the faces of people as they listened to her – just ordinary people who had crowded into a school hall to hear her. Every face, young and old, simple and sophisticated, was rapt, hanging on her words; not because of the words themselves – they were ordinary enough – but because of her. Some quality that came across over and above the words held their attention. A luminosity seemed to fill the school hall, illumining the rapt faces, penetrating into every mind and heart.

When she had finished and the meeting was over, they all wanted to touch her hand; to be physically near her for a moment; to partake of her, as it were. She looked so small and frail and tired standing there, giving herself. Yet this, I reflected, is how we may find salvation. Giving, not receiving; the anti-ad, the dispensing rather than the consuming society; dying in order to live. One old man, not content just to take her hand, bent his grey head down to kiss it. So they do to queens and eminences and great seigneurs. In this particular case, it was a gesture of perfect thankfulness to God – in which I shared – for helping our poor stumbling minds and fearful hearts by showing us his everlasting truth in the guise of one homely face going about his work of love.

The Christian religion finds expression thus, in the love of those who love Christ, more comprehensibly and accessibly than in metaphysical or ethical statements. It is an experience rather than a conclusion, a way of life rather than an ideology; grasped through the imagination rather than understood through the mind, belonging to the realm of spiritual rather than intellectual perception; reaching quite beyond the dimension of words and ideas. As St Augustine found on that wonderful occasion at Ostia with his mother shortly before she died, when they were carried together to somewhere near the very presence of God, and then, returning, found words as clumsy instruments as a surgeon might find a hack-saw, or an artist a house-painter's brush – 'And while we spoke of the eternal Wisdom, longing for it and straining for it with all the strength of our hearts, for one fleeting instant we reached out and touched it. Then, with a sigh, leaving our spiritual harvest bound to it, we returned to the sound of our own speech, in which each word has a beginning and an ending – far, far different from your Word, our Lord, who abides in Himself for ever, yet never grows old and gives new life to all things.'

As it is so beautifully put in the opening chapter of the Fourth Gospel: *And the Word was made flesh, and dwelt among us, full of grace and truth.* The Christian story is simply an end-less presentation of this process of the Word becoming flesh and dwelling gracefully and truthfully among us. Whether in the ultimate silence of the mystic, such as befell St Augustine and his mother – a silence that comprehends all that ever has been, will be and can be said and understood and sensed, from before the beginning of time to beyond its ending. Or

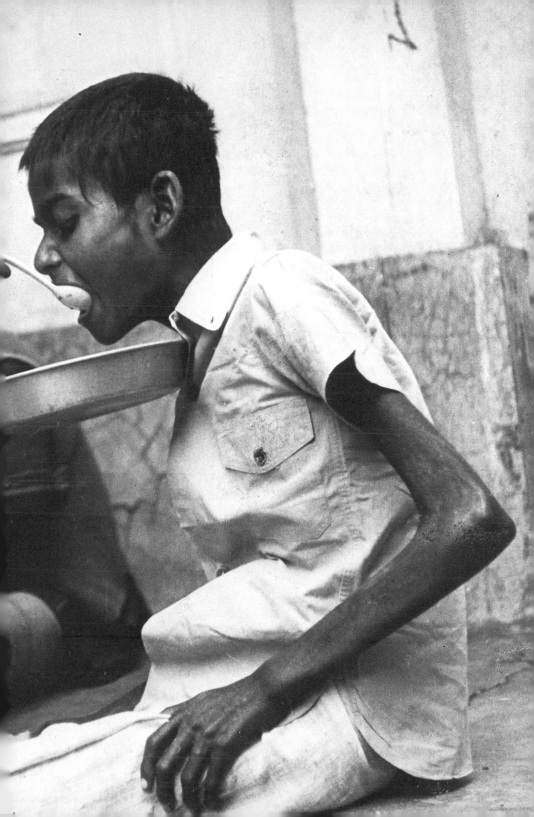

in a Mother Teresa and her Missionaries of Charity going about the world and shining their light in its darkest places. Or in the splendour of artistic creation; in the great cathedrals climbing into the sky to God's greater glory; in the glowing words, the sentient stone and paint, the swelling sounds of music. Or in the solitary soul questing for truth, in the tiniest mechanisms of our mortal existence, as in the universe's illimitable reaches. Or in the beatific soap opera of worship, with its monotonously repeated pleas, confessions and expectations, its *glorias* and its *misereres*, its plainsong and hallelujah choruses; eyes piously downcast, and knees piously kneeling on the world's cold stone. In each and every manifestation of our mortal seeking the immortal, or our temporal seeking the eternal, or our imperfect seeking the perfect. Of men reaching up to God, and God in love and compassion bending down to men.

Each day Mother Teresa meets Jesus; first at the Mass, whence she derives sustenance and strength; then in each needing, suffering soul she sees and tends. They are one and the same Jesus; at the altar and in the streets. Neither exists without the other. We who are imprisoned in history; castaways on the barren shores of time, past, present and to come – we seek another Jesus. A Jesus of history, which is actually a contradiction in terms; like an eternity clock or an infinity tape-measure. Jesus can only exist now; and, in existing now, makes now always. Thus, for Mother Teresa the two commandments – to love God and to love our neighbour – are jointly fulfilled; indeed, inseparable. In her life and work she exemplifies the relation between the two; how, if we do not love God we cannot love our neighbour, and if we do not love our neighbour we cannot love God.

It may strike a contemporary mind as extraordinary that someone like Mother Teresa, in contact all the time with human suffering at its most acute and most desolate, should herself convey such an impression of total serenity, and be so confident of God's love and care for the creatures of his creation. Maybe it is partly this very circumstance which draws to her in an almost magical way those who see and hear her. Suffering crystallizes, as nothing else does, the dilemmas and nightmares of life without God. It is an inflamed nerve which, touched, gives rise to howls of rage and anguish, especially today. Surely, when we can go to the moon, and ride through space faster than light; when our very genes are counted, and our organs replaceable; when we can arrange to eat without growing fat, to copulate without procreating, to flash a gleaming smile without being happy – surely suffering should be banished from our lives. That *we* should have to go on suffering, and watch others suffering, is an outrage; and a deity who, having the power to stop it, still allowed it to continue, would be a monster, not a loving God. So Simone de Beauvoir, watching her mother die in agony of cancer, saw it as 'an unjustifiable violation'; as something 'as violent and unforeseen as an engine stopping in the middle of the sky'. The image is significant. When machines jam and go wrong, we hate them utterly, and look round for a manufacturer or mechanic to curse. In the eyes of those who see men as machines, God is that manufacturer, and the mechanic his priest.

Mother Teresa, of course, sees it quite differently. Suffering and death, to her, are not the breakdown of a machine, but part of the everlasting drama of our relationship with our creator. Far from being an unjustifiable violation, an outrage, they exemplify and enhance our human condition. If ever it were to be possible – as some arrogant contemporary minds are crazy enough to believe – to eliminate suffering, and ultimately death, from our mortal lives, they would not thereby be enhanced, but rather demeaned, to the point that they would become too insignificant, too banal, to be worth living at all. Rather as though, out of humanitarian pity for poor old King Lear, at the end of Act I he were to be given a sedative strong enough to let him sleep through the other four acts. Thereby he would be spared, true, but there would be no play. So for us, too, if the eugenist's dream were ever to be realized – the sick and the old and the mad, all who were infirm and less than physically complete and smooth-working, painlessly eliminated, leaving only the beauty queens and the athletes, the Mensa IQs, and the prize-winners to be our human family – if this ever came to pass (a possibility shudderingly envisaged at some refrigerated Scandinavian bacchanalia, or along the ice-bound corridors of cash), God really would be dead. The only way God ever could die would be if we retreated so far into our egos and our flesh, put between us and him so wide a chasm, that our separation became inexorable. Then, and only then, God would be dead, and the curtain would fall for ever on us and our tiny earth.

It so happened that just when I was thinking about all this *à propos* Mother Teresa, I participated in a television programme about suffering, as a result of which I received hundreds of letters, nearly all of them recounting some experience of

suffering, or of watching over suffering. Just because television, unlike any other means of communication which has
ever existed, reaches more or less everyone, at all social and
mental levels, the correspondence it gives rise to covers a
similarly wide swath. The letter-writers range between near-
illiterates and dons, clergymen, civil servants and the like. In
this particular case, the deep concern felt by one and all broke
through the differing styles and idioms. As between a pro-
fessor's neat missive quoting Blake and the stumbling
scribble of some crippled pensioner there seemed, for once,
little difference; the majesty of the matter at issue dwarfed
variations in the manner and competence of presentation. I
was conscious, turning over these letters, more poignantly
than ever before, of how all of us are at one, if not in our
hopes and desires, then in the scars and bruises we bear, or
have watched with anguish being inflicted on some beloved
flesh – still more agonizedly on some beloved mind, bringing
down the darkness upon it. We can still gather together
round the Cross even though we shut our ears to the words
of the *Man* who died on it.

It was altogether a harrowing correspondence, though
with many beautiful and uplifting accounts of suffering overcome and affliction turned to good purposes – as sometimes
dark clouds which gather turn to glory when the sun sets.
Thus, a lady describes how, through a mental breakdown
suffered some years ago, she became 'a much better person
than I used to be. My fellow patients help me when I am
"down", and I help them when they need it.' In their common affliction they drew together in mutual helpfulness and
love, forming attachments which continued and grew

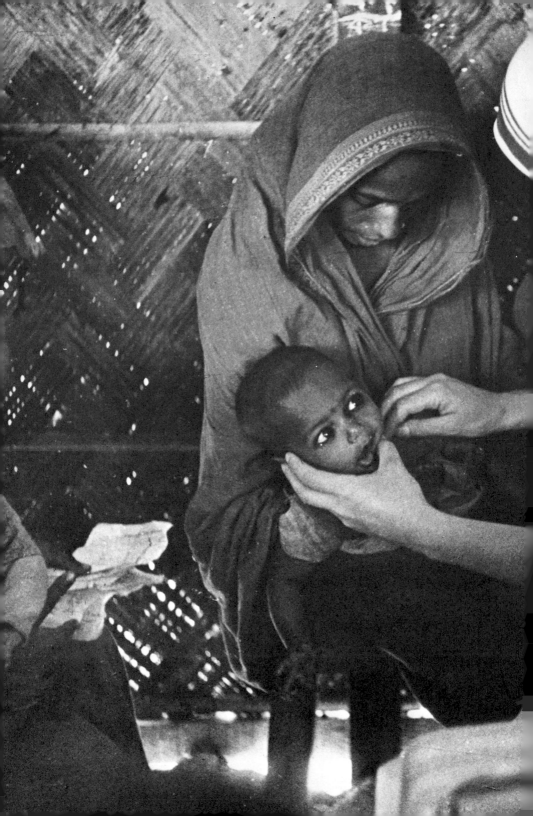

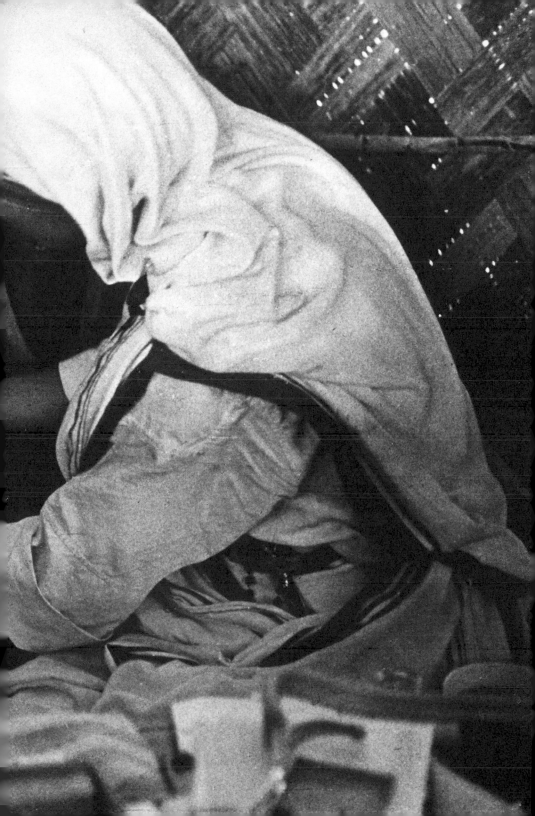

stronger when they emerged from the shadows of their sickness. This, too, is something beautiful for God, shining through the desolation of the drugged faces and listless bodies which haunt one after a visit to a psychiatric ward.

Another lady thanks me for the programme 'which I watched through the mirror of my iron lung'. What fabulous, God-given courage! I who find the confines of my own easeful circumstances an intolerable constriction – how, I ask myself, should I fare in an iron lung? 'It seems to me a wonderful thing,' she goes on, 'that God has taken this evil suffering and overlaid it with so much positive good, the compassion and learning of which you spoke. As for the individual, I think this is one way in which we are made "more than conquerors". Not only do we have strength available to bear the suffering, but we can also make this evil an instrument for good to other people.' Yet another correspondent – a sufferer from muscular dystrophy – describes how, when the doctors told him he must get worse, and he was put on a régime that required swallowing some twenty tablets daily, he took his 'sickness to the Great Physician, and he healed me completely. Since then I've never taken a tablet, and my health is perfect.' 'Suffering,' he concludes, 'I know why I suffered. It was to teach me compassion, and more, it was to keep me humble in the knowledge of his wondrous grace.'

I could go on and on with such quotations, not, heaven knows, with any desire to spread complacency about others' misfortunes; rather, taking pride in belonging to the same human family as these heroic souls – exemplars of the enchanting lines of Blake I often say over to myself when afflicted by a sense of the seeming injustice with which the gifts and pains of life are distributed:

> *Joy and woe are woven fine,*
> *A clothing for the soul divine;*
> *Under every grief and pine*
> *Runs a joy with silken twine.*
> *It is right it should be so;*
> *Man was made for joy and woe;*
> *And when this we rightly know,*
> *Through the world we safely go.*

On the other side, there were some – but by no means as many – letters complaining, with varying degrees of bitterness, of the seemingly pointless suffering which they, or those dear to them, had been forced to endure. Let me give one example. A mother writes of how she had a lovely son who was born a blue baby. Two major heart operations, one when he was five and the other when he was thirteen, overcame some of his disability. He grew into a cheerful youth, won a maths exhibition at Oxford, and altogether 'blossomed and matured'. A last operation, finally to close up the hole in his heart, remained. He had it, returned home; then, a few weeks later, had to return to hospital, where it was discovered that the hole had opened again. One more desperate operation failed, and he died.

'He was just twenty-two,' his mother writes. 'His last words to me in reply to my, "Then I'll see you tomorrow, Ralph," were: "I don't think you will. I'm sorry, Goodbye." Such a firm goodbye, said with closed eyes and ashen face. I went away to take away from him the burden of my concern and sorrow; he sent me away to save me pain.'

'Where is God,' she goes on, 'and why does he allow such cruel things to happen? I have been an agnostic with Christian leanings – so was my son. I felt there was a benign influence in the world, and was happy. . . . Other people have even worse tragedies – though my loss is made more cruel through the tremendous faith and hope I had that my son would one day be well. Had he died when he was a small sick boy I could have cuddled and comforted him, and accepted that he was better off out of this world. But why should he have to go when he had struggled and battled to reach a fine young manhood? He did not want to die. . . . Perhaps I am only thinking of myself, and my son is indeed better off where he is – but how can I *know* this? I can only feel the great desolation that he has gone from this world, leaving a grievous gap in the lives of his parents and his brother. *Where is your God?*'

Where is my God? Dear Mrs ——, he is everywhere; even in the hole in your son's heart, or nowhere. I look out of my window, as I write these words, at a wintry countryside. The bees and the badgers are asleep; the birds perch hungrily on the bare twigs; nature seems dead for ever. Yet not so. Faith tells me that soon the badgers and the bees will awake, the trees load themselves with leaves, the birds sing joyously as they once more build their nests, the dead earth renew itself and wear all the greenery of yet another harvest.

This is a faith easily held. We know – or think we do – that spring will always return. Now I turn my glance from the window into my own heart, seeing there the litter and the dust of wasted years. Old envies not quite spent, old appetites that still could be reanimated, old hopes and desires that flounder on even though whatever outcome they might expect to have has long ago proved illusory. This, too – the interior of my heart – seems a dead landscape. Yet faith tells me that it, likewise, can have a spring in the rebirth promised to us all in the new dispensation which Christ brought to the world. The old envies budding with holy love; the old lusts burning with spiritual appetite; the old hopes and desires finding a new destination in the bright radiance of God's universal love.

Over and above any spring we may know, outside our windows or in our hearts, there is the illimitable sweep of God's concern for his creation and his creatures; comprehending both suffering and beatitude, and transcending both. No one who has been spared – certainly not I – dare say to the afflicted that they are blessed in their affliction, or offer comfort in universal terms for particular griefs. Yet one can dimly see and humbly say that suffering is an integral and essential part of our human drama. That it falls upon one and all in differing degrees and forms whose comparison lies beyond our competence. That it belongs to God's purpose for us here on earth, so that, in the end, all the experience of living has to teach us is to say: Thy will be done. To say it standing before a cross; itself signifying the suffering of God in the person of a Man, and the redemption of a Man in the person of God. The greatest sorrow and the greatest joy co-existing on Golgotha.

All this is said far more cogently and simply by Mother Teresa in one of her smiles or gestures; as I have seen her just lay a hand on the troubled head of a despairing leper, who is thereby at once comforted and reassured. To me, her very existence is likewise comforting and reassuring. Yet I am conscious of, not exactly a reproach – a sense of disappointed expectancy in her attitude. As though she were waiting for something not yet accorded. And, of course, I know exactly what it is – a total commitment to Christ, which, for her, can only be through the Church, and the dispensing from its altars of the Blessed Sacrament.

We talked the matter over, walking by the Serpentine in winter sunshine, among the other strollers, some of them exercising dogs, or, solitary, wearing that inscrutable, aloof look of those who stroll while others work. I took up my well-prepared defensive position behind the Church, whose deficiencies, crumbling barricades and woeful future prospects I expatiated upon, though with little effect. After she had left, I got a letter from her, in her own hand, written, I must suppose, in the night, since her days were taken up wholly with travelling and sometimes six or seven meetings a day. With the letter was a little devotional book by Fr Paul de Jaegher, a Jesuit; very redolent of her, paper-backed, much used, and reaching her, I should imagine, after passing through numerous other hands. There is an inscription to the original owner: 'To Peggy, with the fervent petition that you may become truly "one with Jesus". The Sister of Regina.' I shall keep it always.

Here is the letter:

I am leaving for Paris tomorrow and then for Venezuela on Sunday. I am sure you will pray for me. These days in England have been full with continual sacrifices, or rather the continuation of the Holy Mass. I think I understand you better now. . . . I

don't know why, but you to me are like Nicodemus, and I am
sure the answer is the same – 'Unless you become a little child.'
I am sure you will understand beautifully everything if you
would only 'become' a little child in God's Hands. Your longing
for God is so deep, and yet He keeps Himself away from you.
He must be forcing Himself to do so because He loves you so
much – as to give Jesus to die for you and for me. Christ is
longing to be your Food. Surrounded with fullness of living food
you allow yourself to starve. The personal love Christ has for
you is infinite; the small difficulty you have re His Church is
finite. Overcome the finite with the infinite. Christ has created
you because He wanted you. I know what you feel – terrible
longing with dark emptiness. And yet He is the one in love with
you. . . . I am sure you will like the book. This is one of the books
I can read often, and it is always new and fresh. I am leaving with
a happy heart that Jesus will soon have one more little tabernacle
– made by the Missionaries of Charity in London. I hope the
blessing will take place on the 8th December. It would be lovely
if the Cardinal came for Holy Mass, but I do not know if one
can ask him. But I feel that if Jesus can come surely the Cardinal
can come also.

Needless to say, the Cardinal came, and the house – in
Southall – was duly consecrated; so that now London, like
Calcutta, has its Missionaries of Charity, needing them no
less.

When Mother Teresa first announced her intention of
opening a house of the Missionaries of Charity in London,
the general expectation was that in a matter of some six
months or so arrangements would be completed. Actually,

everything was settled in less than two weeks. A house was bought in Southall, where many Indian immigrants are living; the minimum essential alterations were made, and the chapel was prepared for the first Mass. Mother Teresa and a small contingent of Sisters under Sister Frederick insisted on moving into the house before it was, in ordinary terms, habitable. Ordinary terms, for her, have no validity. She led a party of willing helpers in scrubbing the house from top to bottom. As usual, helpers from the locality and the Co-Workers appeared on the scene as and when required, and by 8 December all was ready. I gathered that, to achieve this result, it had been necessary to press the builders working in the house somewhat hard; to the point that, for one whole day, rather than risk touching off their exasperation by emerging, Mother Teresa and the Sisters thought it more prudent to stay in one of the back rooms, singing hymns, praying and meditating together.

Cardinal Heenan consecrated the chapel and celebrated the first Mass. It was the most beautiful service I have ever attended. As it happened, the electricity workers' go-slow was on, so we had only candle light, which somehow added to the mystery and majesty of the proceedings. I thought of the vain battle of greed which had plunged much of London in darkness that day, and of how such battles and such darkness are the stuff of history and the fruit of our un-redeemed mortal natures. Here in this front parlour of a small suburban house, where an altar and a cross had been set up (provided, actually, by some Anglican nuns), a little clearing was made in the dark jungle of the human will. I was enchanted to be there.

The face of the man who read the Gospel had a singular beauty; the Cardinal in his vestments looked as I had never seen him look before, with some extra dimension of luminosity about him; the Sisters sang their hymns, using the cyclostyled hymnal I knew from the morning Masses in Calcutta. The chapel was the only room in the house that could be said to be furnished. It was the Lord's room, and so alone mattered. Though, I reflected, our insane ways were causing London to be blacked out, Mother Teresa had shone a light there brighter than all the lost lights together; a light which could never be extinguished.

I am very conscious of the inadequacy of my effort to convey in words more than a hazy and inadequate impression of this woman of God and her Co-Workers. Often in the course of it I have echoed the prayer St Paul asked the Christians of Colossae to offer on his behalf – that God would open a door of utterance. It will be for posterity to decide whether she is a saint. I only say of her that in a dark time she is a burning and a shining light; in a cruel time, a living embodiment of Christ's gospel of love; in a godless time, the Word dwelling among us, full of grace and truth. For this, all who have the inestimable privilege of knowing her, or knowing of her, must be eternally grateful.

APPENDIX

CONSTITUTION

1. 'The International Association of Co-Workers of Mother Teresa' consists of men, women, young people and children of all religions and denominations throughout the world, who seek to love God in their fellow men, through whole hearted free service to the poorest of the poor of all castes and creeds, and who wish to unite themselves in a spirit of prayer and sacrifice with the·work of Mother Teresa and the Missionaries of Charity.

2. Mother Teresa's desire is that all Co-Workers, Sisters and Brothers, and the poor unite themselves to each other in prayer and sacrifice:

A. By helping people recognize God in the person of the poor.

B. By helping people love God better through works of charity and service to the poor.

C. By uniting the Missionaries of Charity and Co-Workers throughout the world in prayer and sacrifice.

D. By keeping the family spirit.

E. By fostering aid between various countries and by eliminating duplication of effort and aid for individual centres of the Missionaries of Charity.

3.   By 'the poor' is meant those who do not have enough to eat, whose living conditions are incompatible with the dignity of the human person, and who are seriously deprived, materially, spiritually or socially, in relation to their neighbours. While hearing the cries of the poor, the Co-Workers will have a special concern for those who are unwanted and unloved.

4.   All Co-Workers express their love of God through service to the poor, as Jesus Christ himself has said:

> 'Whatever you did to the least of these my brethren, you did it to Me' (Matthew 25:40).
>
> 'For I was hungry, and you gave Me to eat;
> I was thirsty, and you gave Me to drink;
> I was homeless, and you took Me in;
> naked and you clothed Me;
> sick and you visited Me;
> in prison and you came to see Me' (Matthew 25:35).

5.   While remaining sensitive and responsive to the needs of the poor who are near to them, the Co-Workers of Mother Teresa give their support to Mother Teresa and to her Missionaries of Charity in their Mission of love to the poorest of the poor wherever they are found, and thus share in the 'whole hearted free service to the poor' which the Sisters and Brothers vow to God.

6.   They recognize the dignity, the individuality and the infinite value of every human life.

7.   The keynote of the giving is Love and Service.

8.   The Co-Workers of Mother Teresa recognize that all the goods of this world – including gifts of mind and body, advantages of birth and education – are the free gifts of God, and that no one has a right to a superfluity of wealth while others are dying of starvation,

and suffering from every kind of want. They seek to right this grave injustice by the exercise of voluntary poverty and the sacrifices of luxuries in their way of life.

9. At the same time and in the same spirit, Co-Workers of Mother Teresa make available to the Missionaries of Charity whatever time and material help are within their power to provide.

10. Co-Workers of Mother Teresa unite in prayer with the Missionaries of Charity by saying the following prayer daily:

Make us worthy, Lord, to serve our fellow men throughout the world who live and die in poverty and hunger. Give them, through our hands, this day their daily bread, and by our understanding love give Peace and Joy.

Lord, make me a channel of Thy peace, that where there is hatred I may bring love; that where there is wrong, I may bring the spirit of forgiveness; that where there is discord, I may bring harmony; that where there is error, I may bring truth; that where there is doubt, I may bring faith; that where there is despair, I may bring hope; that where there are shadows, I may bring light; that where there is sadness, I may bring joy.

Lord, grant that I may seek rather to comfort than to be comforted; to understand than to be understood; to love than to be loved; for it is by forgetting self that one finds; it is by dying that one awakens to eternal life. Amen.

11. Co-Workers should emulate the spirit of poverty and humility of the Missionaries of Charity and should avoid unnecessary expenses at their meetings and should conduct all their business affairs with economy and austerity.

12. As the Missionaries of Charity give whole hearted free service to the poor, so the Co-Workers also and all those in office will give their whole hearted free service.

13. In accordance with Mother Teresa's wish, Co-Workers throughout the world should maintain contact with one another and exchange ideas and information through the INTERNATIONAL COMMITTEE:

PRESIDENT

Mother M. Teresa M.C. (Foundress)

PERMANENT SECRETARY

Sister M. Frederick M.C.
(Missionaries of Charity, 54A Lower Circular Road,
Calcutta 16, India)

CHAIRMAN

Mrs Ann Blaikie
(2 Silvermere, Byfleet Road, Cobham, Surrey, England)

VICE-CHAIRMEN

(one per country appointed by Governing Body)

LINK SICK AND SUFFERING CO-WORKERS

Mlle Jacqueline de Decker
(Rue Prince Albert, Antwerp, Belgium)

14. GOVERNING BODY According to circumstances and need the President, Chairman and Permanent Secretary and their successors in office shall be the Governing Body, and may omit and amend and add to the rules of the Constitution of 'The International Association of Co-Workers of Mother Teresa'. No change of aim or constitution may be made by any one else in any country. All officers are voluntary.

15. YEARLY NEWS BULLETIN

(a) Vice-Chairmen will send to the Chairman by a stated date a short summary of projects undertaken and aid given by their country during the previous year, for inclusion in the Annual Bulletin. Activities undertaken by children should be mentioned separately.

(b) The Bulletin will contain:

    (i) News of the Missionaries of Charity.

    (ii) Summaries as in (a) above.

    (iii) Obituaries among the Co-Workers, Sisters and Brothers (these should be sent to the Chairman as they occur).

    (iv) Addresses of the Vice-Chairmen.

    (v) Any other matters.

(c) The Vice-Chairmen will be responsible for getting copies made in their own countries and for the distribution of the same.

16. PRAYER CARDS All are asked to use the prayer cards and to meditate on one chosen passage for a few minutes before the meetings.

17. DAY OF PRAYER A Day of Prayer and Thanksgiving will be held on the 7th October, throughout the world, being the day on which the Society of the Missionaries of Charity was founded in 1950. On that day all are asked to unite with the Sisters and Brothers in giving thanks to God.

18. BRANCHES OF THE ASSOCIATION Branches of the Association are established in a number of countries. Normally Co-Workers share in Mother Teresa's work through membership of a small group or as an individual.

19. SICK AND SUFFERING CO-WORKERS The sick and those unable to join in activities may become a close Co-Worker of an individual Sister or Brother by offering their prayer and suffering for such Sister or Brother.

20. SEAL The Missionaries of Charity seal will be used only on official correspondence.

CHRONOLOGICAL TABLE

27 August 1910 Born of Albanian parents at Skopje, Yugo-slavia. There were three children, one boy and two girls. She attended the government school. Whilst at school she became a member of the Sodality. At that time the Yugoslav Jesuits had accepted to work in the Calcutta Archdiocese. The first group arrived in Calcutta on 30 December 1925. One of them was sent to Kurseong. From there he sent enthusiastic letters about the Bengal Mission field. Those letters were read regularly to the Sodalists. Young Agnes was one of the Sodalists who volunteered for the Bengal Mission. She was put in touch with the Loreto nuns in Ireland, as they were working in the Calcutta Archdiocese.

29 November 1928 She was sent to Loreto Abbey, Rathfarn-ham, Dublin, Ireland and from there to India to begin her noviciate in Darjeeling.

1929–48 She taught geography at the St Mary's High School in Calcutta. For some years she was a Principal of the school. She was also in charge of the Daughters of St Anne, the Indian religious order attached to the Loreto Sisters.

10 September 1946 'A day of decision.' Mother Teresa re-quested permission from her Superior to live alone outside the cloister and to work in the Calcutta slums. Her request was taken to Rome and approved.

8 August 1948 Mother Teresa laid aside the Loreto habit and clothed herself in the white sari, with blue border and cross on the shoulder. She went to Patna for three months to the American Medical Missionary Sisters for an intensive nursing training. By Christmas she was back in Calcutta and living with the Little Sisters of the Poor.

21 December 1948 She obtained permission to open her first slum school.

February 1949 She moved into a flat in a private house owned by the Gomes family.

19 March 1949 The first recruit arrived, a young Bengali girl.

7 October 1950 The new congregation of the Missionaries of Charity was approved and instituted in Calcutta, and from there spread throughout India.

25 March 1963 The Archbishop of Calcutta blessed the beginnings of a new branch, the Missionary Brothers of Charity.

1 February 1965 The Missionaries of Charity became a society of pontifical right.

1965 To Venezuela to open a centre near Caracas.

1967 To Ceylon to open in Colombo.

1968 To Tanzania to open in Tabora, and to Rome to open in the slums of that city.

1969 To Bourke, Australia to open a centre for Aborigines.

26 March 1969 The International Association of Co-Workers of Mother Teresa was affiliated to the order of the Missionaries of Charity and the constitution of the association was presented to His Holiness Pope Paul VI and received his blessing.

April 1970 To Melbourne.

July 1970 To Amman, Jordan.

8 December 1970 A Noviciate was opened in London to train novices from Europe and the Americas.

6 January 1971 She was awarded the Pope John XXIII Peace Prize by Pope Paul VI.

16 October 1971 Kennedy International Award Winner for 'outstanding service to mankind.'